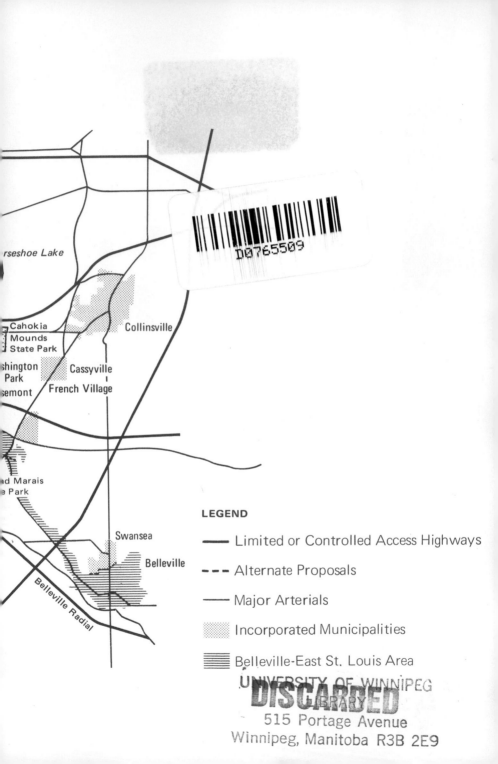

rseshoe Lake

Cahokia
Mounds
State Park

shington
Park
semont

Cassyville

French Village

Collinsville

d Marais
e Park

Swansea

Belleville

Belleville Radial

LEGEND

—— Limited or Controlled Access Highways

- - - Alternate Proposals

—— Major Arterials

▧ Incorporated Municipalities

≡ Belleville-East St. Louis Area

THE POLITICS OF BELLEVILLE

THE
POLITICS
OF
BELLEVILLE

A Profile of the Civil Community

DANIEL J. ELAZAR

Temple
University
Press
PHILADELPHIA

For Alan, Arthur, Jerry, Lee and Rubin and the other members
of the Beatrice Arms Cooperative Society

Temple University Press, Philadelphia 19122
© 1971 by Temple University. All rights reserved
Published 1971
Printed in the United States of America

International Standard Book Number: 0-87722-013-1
Library of Congress Catalog Card Number: 70-182890

Rear endpaper map courtesy Belleville City Planning Commission

CONTENTS

Preface   vii

1 Themes and Theses   3
    The Civil Community   4
    The Continuing Frontier   5
    Political Culture and the Cultural Streams   9
    Sectionalism   15
    Federalism   16
    The Progression of Generations   16

2 The Setting   20
    The Physical Basis of Belleville's Community   20
    The Socio-Religious Basis of Belleville's Politics   27
    The Economic Basis of Belleville's Independence   36

3 The Constitution of the Civil Community   46
    The Limits of the Civil Community   46
    The Evolution of the Formal Structure   58
    Belleville's Constitution: The Other Ingredients   66
    Local Politics and Patterns of Partisan Allegiance   71

4 Public Institutions and the Structure of Power   78
       The Oligarchy and Its Span of Control   78
       The Character and Composition of the Oligarchy   86
       The Structure and Functions of the City Government 93
       Politics in the Other Governments   102
       Intergovernmental Relations   107

5 The Course of Postwar Reform   118
       The Calhoun Years   118
       Continuing Reform in the Post-Calhoun Years   127
       Reforming the Whole Civil Community   132
       The Future of Local Reform   134

6 Oligarchy and Reform in Belleville   135

Appendix A: The Method of Exploration   144

Appendix B: Selected Bibliography   150

Index   155

PREFACE

The Politics of Belleville is the first of a series of "political maps" of the medium-sized metropolitan communities of the Upper Mississippi Valley now being prepared in the Center for the Study of Federalism at Temple University to illuminate the structure and functions of a relatively new urban phenomenon on the American scene, both within and outside of the country's great metropolitan regions. These political maps are designed to present a picture of community politics in those medium-sized metropolitan communities during the half-generation following World War II, roughly 1946 to 1961, when the thrust of America's response to the problems of the contemporary city was concentrated on the local plane.

A "political map," in the sense used herein, is an outline of the structure of the community as a whole and the patterns of political behavior that animate and give meaning to that structure. It is concerned with the geographic, historical, cultural, and socio-economic patterns that affect the political system, as well as with "politics" per se.

While this book stands alone as a description of the Belleville civil community, it is designed as part of the larger "Cities of the Prairie" series and is best appreciated in light of the more analytical volumes in that series, the first of which is the author's *Cities of the Prairie: The Metropolitan Frontier and American Politics* (New York: Basic Books, 1970). Since the bulk of the analytical treatment of urban politics and its meaning is confined to the general volumes, this book is primarily a descriptive account of the political patterns in Belleville. As such, it provides a convenient statement of some of the empirical data on which the analytical volumes are based, presented in more detail than is possible in the longer works. At the same time, it stands alone as an effort to contribute to the comparative study of urban communities. The description and analysis of Belleville's political system presented in the following pages are built on concepts fully discussed in *Cities of the Prairie*. For clarity's sake, they are briefly delineated in Chapter 1.

The sources for the data in the following pages are included in an appendix at the end of this book. For the sake of brevity, and in order to protect the sources of the material, specific citations have been omitted in the body of the report. A methodological appendix, adapted from a more extensive one in *Cities of the Prairie*, is included for those so inclined, which explains the manner in which the information presented straightforwardly in the following pages was gathered and authenticated.

The study of which this book is a part was initiated under the auspices of the Institute of Government and Public Affairs of the University of Illinois. It has since been taken over by the Center for the Study of Federalism of Temple University, under whose auspices this book was completed. Thanks are due the Institute and Gilbert Y. Steiner, then its director, for supporting the research for an initial draft of this book. Grateful acknowledgement is also due Seymour Z. Mann, then of the Institute of Public Administration and Metropolitan

Affairs, Southern Illinois University, and his staff for their assistance during the author's stay in the Belleville area. The many people in the Belleville civil community who gave of their time to further the goals of this study are acknowledged with particular thanks. The staff of the Center for the Study of Federalism of Temple University has been of great assistance as always. Special acknowledgement is due Benjamin R. Schuster, research assistant in the Center, for his attention to the numerous details that must be taken care of in the final stages of preparing a manuscript for publication.

THE POLITICS OF BELLEVILLE

CHAPTER ONE

THEMES
AND
THESES

Belleville, Illinois is a medium-sized civil community "buried" within the St. Louis "Standard Metropolitan Statistical Area" (SMSA). To the outside observer familiar with the usual quantified picture of American urbanization, Belleville is hardly visible as a city in its own right. Yet "up close" it emerges as an urban community as fully independent and independent-minded as any free-standing city miles from a metropolis. More than that, it is easily identified as something of a minor metropolis, the center of an urban area hardly less definable than any SMSA.

In both respects, Belleville is typical of several hundred American cities today, hidden by convention in the officially recognized "metropolitan areas" where they are lumped together with large central cities and small suburbs into an indistinguishable mass of colossal size, even though they actually function as relatively autonomous communities that command the primary, if not the exclusive, local loyalties of the overwhelming majority of their residents. An understanding of the Bellevilles of the United States, how and why they are and remain independent civil communities within great metropolitan regions, and what makes them tick, is crucial to understanding the nature of American urbanization, and perhaps more important, to understanding how an urbanized and metropolitanized America can possibly retain human scale in its social and political life.

The Civil Community

The central thesis of the "Cities of the Prairie" studies is that the American urban community is not necessarily defined politically by the boundaries of either its SMSA or the particular central city after which it is named. Even the area included in the municipal boundaries of the latter is, in most cases, organized politically in a more complex manner than that. In fact, we can understand the American urban place as a community only when we view it as a "civil community," a term developed by the author to better describe the way in which an urbanized area that frequently extends beyond the formal city limits of most central cities is bound together as a meaningful political system.[1]

A civil community may be defined as the organized sum of the political institutions functioning in a given locality to provide the bundle of governmental services and activities that can be manipulated locally to serve local needs in light of the local value system. Every civil community is composed of at least six elements: (1) the formally established local governments serving it, such as the municipal governments, the county, and the school and special districts; (2) the local agencies of the state and federal governments, insofar as they are adjuncts of the local community, existing primarily to serve it, such as the local branches of the state employment office and the post office; (3) the public nongovernmental bodies serving local governmental or quasi-governmental purposes, such as the chamber of commerce and the community welfare council; (4) the political parties and factions functioning within the civil community to organize political competition; (5) the system of interest groups functioning in the local political arena to represent the various local interests; and (6) the body of written constitutional material and unwritten tradition serving as a framework within which sanctioned political action must take place and as a check against unsanctioned political behavior. The civil community and its components are schematically portrayed in Figure 1.

Belleville is as close an approximation of the civil community as an ideal type as is likely to be found: a subcounty area centered on a core city but extending beyond the municipal boundaries. Moreover, it represents the "hard case," a discrete civil community whose identity is clear even though it is located within a great metropolitan region which robs it of recognition by outsiders for the entity it is. The major thrust of this book is the delineation of Belleville as a civil community.

The Continuing Frontier

The second important thesis advanced in this study holds that American historical development is best reflected in the national response to three successive frontiers, each of which has demanded that Americans come to grips with an untamed element of nature and, by taming it, reorganize their society.[2] Since the opening of settlement in 1607, the American frontier has passed through three stages. First came the *rural-land* frontier—the classic American frontier described by the historians—lasting roughly from the seventeenth through the nineteenth centuries. It was characterized by the westward movement of a basically rural population interested in settling and exploiting the land and by the development of a socio-economic system based on agricultural and extractive pursuits in both its urban and rural components.

Early in the nineteenth century, the rural-land frontier gave birth to the *urban-industrial* frontier, which began in the Northeast and spread westward, in the course of which it transformed the nation into an industrial society settled in cities and dedicated to the spread of a new technology as the

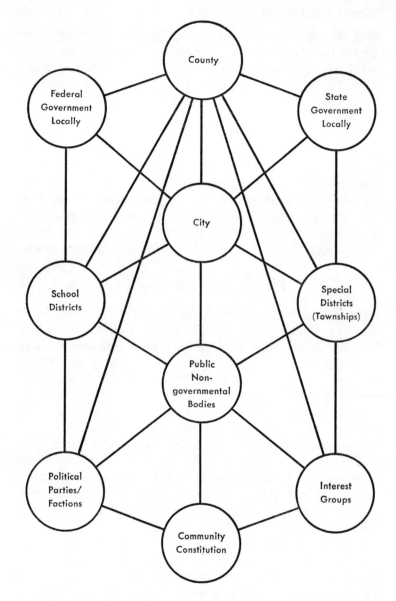

FIG. 1. The civil community and its components

primary source of the nation's economic and social forms. The dominant characteristic of this frontier was the transformation of cities from service centers or workshops for the rural areas into independent centers of opportunity, producers of new wealth, and social innovators possessing internally generated reasons for existence and growth. At first overlapping the land frontier, the urban-industrial frontier became dominant by the last third of the century.

By the mid-twentieth century, the urban-industrial frontier had given birth, in turn, to the *metropolitan-technological* frontier, characterized by the radical reordering of an industrial society through rapidly changing technologies and a settlement pattern that encourages the diffusion of an urbanized population within large metropolitan regions. These radically new technologies, ranging from atomic energy and automation to synthetics and cybernetics, and the accompanying suburbanization of the population have generated further changes in the nation's social and economic forms in accord with their new demands. Like the first two frontier stages, the metropolitan-technological frontier has also moved from east to west since the 1920s, becoming dominant nationally after World War II.

Each successive frontier stage has opened new vistas and new avenues of opportunity for the American people, in the development of new economic activities, the creation of new settlement patterns, and the mastery of new social problems growing out of the collision of old patterns and new demands. Consequently, each has generated new political concerns revolving around the accommodation of the challenges and opportunities within the civil society.

Like most American cities, Belleville has experienced all three frontier stages, adapting to each in its own way, but generally following classic lines in each case (Table 1). Its land frontier stage was relatively brief. It was founded as a service center for the surrounding agricultural area in the manner of most American cities and, once coal mining was

TABLE 1

Frontiers and Generations in the United States and Belleville

Year	Generation	Frontier Stage	Belleville Development
1810	6	Rural-Land	
			1814 Founding of Belleville and creation of first local, state, and federal political institutions
			1819 Incorporation of Belleville as a village to complete founding process
1820			
1830	7		1830 Beginning of German immigration, creation of indigenous culture
1840			
1850		Urban-Industrial	1850 Incorporation as city, completing institutionalization of new government services of the late 1840s
			1857- Enlargement and professionalization of
1860	8		1867 city services in response to opening of urban frontier
1870			
			1876 Reincorporation of Belleville under Illinois Cities and Villages Act
1880			
1890	9		1890 Institution of township system
			1890- Transition to modern municipal services
1900			1905
1910			
			1916- Introduction of new institutional factors
			1917 to redefine boundaries of the civil community
1920	10		
1930			
			1933- Depression public works programs to re-
1940			1941 build community's public infrastructure
		Metropolitan-Technological	1946 Establishment of Junior College and transition at Scott AFB, completing changes of tenth generation
			1949 Reform movement, marking transition to metropolitan frontier
1950			
1960	11		1960 Institutionalization of reform movement
1970			

begun, serviced that extractive manifestation of the land frontier as well. About the time that the surrounding territory was fully settled, and the settlers rooted in, Belleville made the transition to the urban-industrial frontier with agriculturally based industries abetting the shift. By the turn of the century Belleville was an exemplary version of the small industrial city on the outer periphery of America's main industrial region, a beneficiary of the urban-industrial frontier without being deeply involved in pioneering on it.

Belleville's location within commuting range of St. Louis virtually guaranteed it a place on the metropolitan-technological frontier, while the system it had developed in its successful adaptation to the earlier frontier stages was invaluable in enabling the civil community to assimilate most of the impact of the new frontier into established local channels. In a real sense, this book deals with Belleville's political responses to the metropolitan-technological frontier, focusing on the half-generation after World War II, the frontier's "take-off" period.

Political Culture and the Cultural Streams

The third major thesis advanced in this study deals with the influence on local political systems of cultural streams developed on the eastern seaboard during the colonial period, or brought from the Old World.[3] The basic patterns of culture, in Belleville and every other American community, were set during the period of the rural-land frontier by three great streams of American migration that began on the east coast and moved westward after the colonial period. Each stream moved, in the persons of the westward migrants, from east to west along more or less fixed paths, following lines of least resistance which generally led them due west from the immediately previous area of settlement. The migrants coming from the eastern seaboard or the Old World to settle the United States west of the Appalachians brought with them distinctive cultural patterns derived from their countries or regions of origin and often rooted in their ethnic and religious backgrounds.

In their new places of settlement, the various ethnic and religious groups aggregated with one another on the basis of their common socio-cultural characteristics. In some cases, these aggregations embraced entire ethnic or "nationality" groups, but in many cases they reflected cultural differences that cut across such groups even in the "Old Country." Since these groups moved as streams across the continent, they may be called "cultural streams" and their subdivisions, "cultural currents."

Fifteen such streams can be identified in the United States, divided into three general groupings. Three native streams developed in the course of the colonial period in American history: the Yankee stream, emerging out of the Puritan settlement of New England; the Middle stream, developing out of the commercially based pluralism of the Middle States; and the Southern stream, emerging out of the plantation and slaveholding South. These were supplemented in the eighteenth and nineteenth centuries by nine non-native streams that integrated with them. The North Sea stream (consisting of those people from Calvinist Britain and Europe plus Scandinavia), the Jewish stream, and the Anglo-Canadian stream (essentially the North Sea stream as filtered through English Canada) all integrated with the Yankee stream. The English stream (consisting of non-Puritan English and Welsh), the Continental stream (essentially Western and Middle Europeans), and the Irish streams integrated with the Middle stream. The Mediterranean stream (principally Italians and Greeks), the Eastern European stream, and the French Canadian stream shared the same characteristics as the Southern stream although, because they settled in different places, they did not integrate with it.

Finally, three streams developed entirely outside of the mainstream of American life: the Afro-American stream, whose

TABLE 2

Modal Characteristics and Interrelationships of Cultural Streams

Streams			Modal characteristics
Native stream	*Non-Native stream*	*Excluded stream*	
Yankee	North Sea Jewish Anglo-Canadian		Calvinistic Protestant, Congregational, or Free Church Entrepreneurial but community-oriented, middle class, Republican, fiercely loyal as a group to one party, or fiercely independent
Middle	English Continental Irish	Oriental	Catholic or hierarchical liturgical Protestant; Individualist, multi-class, entrepreneurial. Mixed party loyalties
Southern	Mediterranean Eastern European French Canadian	Hispanic Afro-American	Single dominant religion or "color"; individualistic but kinship-oriented, originally peasant or working class, overt ethnic identity, Democratic

origins are fully as native as those of the first three streams; the Hispanic stream (Mexicans, Puerto Ricans, and Cubans); and the Oriental stream (Chinese, Japanese, and Filipinos) that have begun to integrate only in our own time. These streams, their modal characteristics and their interrelationships, are schematically portrayed in Table 2.

Part and parcel of each cultural stream is a particular pattern of orientation to political action: a political culture which can be understood as a separate variable in the life of the local community. The basic political styles, demands, and values which shape the political processes and the handling of political issues in the civil community are, in large measure,

determined by the local political culture as it has developed
and become manifest over time. Consequently, an understanding of the factors which give the same objective phenomena
a unique local meaning—the crucial factors in understanding
a particular local political system—rest upon identification of
the local political cultural patterns and their concrete political
manifestations.

In the United States, three basic political subcultures have
emerged: the moralistic, out of the Yankee stream and those
allied with it; the individualistic, out of the Middle stream
and those allied with it; and the traditionalistic, out of the
Southern stream and those which share its basic characteristics.
The character of each of these subcultures has been described
elsewhere by this writer.[4] Here it is sufficient to note that
Belleville's political culture is the product of a synthesis of
the traditionalistic and individualistic subcultures, with the
latter dominant. This means that Bellevillians, in line with
their individualistic political culture, emphasize the conception
of the democratic order as a marketplace, although, given
their traditionalistic underpinnings, one relatively well controlled by a recognized élite. In their view, government is
instituted for strictly utilitarian reasons, to handle only those
functions directly demanded by the people it is created to
serve. A government need not have any direct concern with
questions of the "good society" except insofar as it may be
used to advance some common conception of the good society
formulated outside the political arena, just as it serves other
functions. Since Belleville's political culture emphasizes the
centrality of private concerns, it places a premium on limiting
community intervention—whether governmental or nongovernmental—into private activities to the minimum necessary to
keep the marketplace in proper working order. In general,
government action is to be restricted to those areas, primarily
in the economic realm, which encourage private initiative and
widespread access to the marketplace for those within the
civil community.

The character of political participation in Belleville also reflects the individualistic-traditionalistic synthesis. Electoral politics and office holding are viewed, in the individualistic manner, as just another means by which individuals may improve themselves socially and economically. In this sense politics is a "business" like any other that competes for talent and offers rewards to those who take it up as a career. Those individuals who choose political careers may rise by providing the governmental services demanded of them and, in turn, may expect to be adequately compensated for their efforts. Interpretations of officeholders' obligations under this arrangement vary among individuals within the local political system. Where the norms are high, as in Belleville, such people are expected to provide high-quality government services for the general public in the best possible manner in return for the status and economic rewards considered their due. Some who choose political careers clearly commit themselves to such norms; others believe that an officeholder's primary responsibility is to serve himself and those who have supported him directly, favoring them even at the expense of others. In many respects, the postwar struggle for reform in Belleville described in this book was a struggle between those who held the former and latter views. At the same time, traditionalistic values encourage the established élites to participate in the governance of Belleville through means other than electoral politics, and their right to do so is accepted by politicians and public alike.

Political life in Belleville is based on a system of mutual obligations rooted in personal relationships. While this system of mutual obligations is harnessed, to some extent, through the political parties which serve as "business corporations" dedicated to providing the organization necessary to maintain it, the traditionalistic aspects of Belleville's political culture function to weaken the role of party within the politics of the civil community. This has led to an important distinction locally. Political regularity is indispensable because it is the

means for coordinating individual enterprise in the political
arena and it is the one way of preventing individualism in
politics from running wild. The ordinary politician in Belleville
can succeed politically, not by dealing with issues in some exceptional way or by accepting some concept of good government and then striving to implement it, but by maintaining his
place in the system of mutual obligations. He can do this only
by operating according to the norms of his particular party
or faction, to the exclusion of other political considerations.
Members of the other élites, however, are less bound by party
considerations *as long as they confine their political interests
to the civil community.* Belleville's political culture encourages
the maintenance of a party system that is competitive, but
not overly so, in the pursuit of office. Its politicians are interested in office as a means of controlling the distribution of the
favors or rewards of government rather than as a means of
exercising governmental power for programmatic ends.

Since their political culture eschews ideological concerns in
its "business-like" conception of politics, both politicians and
citizens in Belleville look upon normal political activity as a
specialized field, essentially the province of professionals and
those "entitled" to speak for the community, of minimum and
passing concern to laymen, and no place for amateurs to play
an active role. Furthermore, there is a strong tendency among
the public to believe that party politics is a tainted—if necessary—business, better left to those who are willing to compromise themselves by engaging in it. In part, this explains
why there is likely to be an easy attitude toward the limits of
the politicians' perquisites. Since a fair amount of violation
of legal restrictions or limitations is expected in the normal
course of things, there is relatively little popular excitement
when any is found unless it is of an extraordinary character.
It is as if the public is willing to pay a surcharge for services
rendered and rebels only when it feels the surcharge has
become too heavy. This, too, can be seen in Belleville's reform
movement and its causes.

In accordance with Belleville's political culture, its public officials are committed to "giving the public what it wants," and are normally not willing to initiate new programs or open up new areas of government activity on their own recognizance. They will do so when they perceive an overwhelming public demand for them to act, but only then. In a sense, their willingness to expand the functions of government is based on an extension of the quid pro quo "favor" system which serves as the central core of their political relationships, with new services the reward they give the public for placing them in office.

Belleville reflects both the individualistic and traditionalistic political cultures in its ambivalence about the place of bureaucracy in the political order. In one sense, the bureaucratic method of operation flies in the face of the combination of government by élites with the political "favor" system that is central to its political process. At the same time, the virtues of organizational efficiency appear substantial to those seeking to master the market. Belleville has met this problem by unionization of the public employees within the framework of the favor system, which allows for the organizational continuity required by modern government while keeping the entire organization within the political environment.

Sectionalism

A fourth major thesis underlying this book deals with the influence of sectionalism on American urbanization and, most specifically, the way in which the country is divided into three great spheres: the greater Northeast, the greater South, and the greater West, which establish the framework for rural, urban, and metropolitan development in the United States. Belleville, located at the point where the three spheres overlap, has been substantially influenced by all three. The character of those influences and the way they have been synthesized locally are discussed in particular detail in Chapter 2. Sectionalism, as such, remains a minor chord in this book, though not an insignificant one.[5]

Federalism

Also underlying this book is the conceptualization of the American federal system which the author and his colleagues have presented elsewhere and which is applied to the urban scene in Chapter 9 of *Cities of the Prairie*.[6] Running through the picture of Belleville which is presented is the idea that Belleville is inextricably woven into the federal-state-local-private partnership which is American federalism and that both its autonomy and its dependence are contingent on its place within the federal system.

The Progression of Generations

Finally, this book is predicated upon a generational theory of political behavior which the author has described more fully in *Toward a Generational Theory of American Politics*.[7] This theory holds that there is a pattern of social challenges and political responses that is reenacted in every polity over the course of every generation. A particular polity's pattern of challenges and responses is so fixed by its historical beginnings that more or less discrete political generations develop to create a progression of events in a visible (though obviously not rigid) pattern over time.

The United States is no exception. In fact, it offers one of the most spectacular examples of the progression of generations because its beginnings were so decisive and its history has been so well documented from the very first. In the first third of the seventeenth century, groups of young adults settled virgin territory at key points and in that way initiated the series of generational progressions with what was, for all intents and purposes, a free hand. As they grew older, they passed from the scene of activity at roughly the same time, allowing their sons (or newcomers of their sons' generation) to occupy the vital positions in their societies' social, economic, cultural, religious, and political life, initiating a process of transition that has persisted into the present eleventh generation of American history. At the same time, those same men continued to contribute in their retirement by shaping the ideas and outlook of their sons' sons; hence the forging of the three-generational "package" which continues to be renewed.

Within each generational time span there is a more or less regular progression of political events revolving around the development of that generation's challenge and its response to that challenge. Nationally, the "border" between the old and new generations is marked by one or more decisive political actions whose characteristic feature is the simultaneous completion of the major responses of the old generation and the opening of opportunity for the new one. The first half of the new generation is a time for recognizing the generational challenge and developing and testing proposals for political action to meet that challenge. At the same time, it is a period of population change as old voters and leaders pass from the scene of political activity and new ones come onto it. During that period there occur the generation's "critical elections" that either change the majority party by breaking up its coalition or reaffirm its majority status by reintegrating that coalition. After the second of the critical elections, the second half of the generation begins with a great spurt of governmental innovation on the national plane designed to respond to the now-recognized challenge that lasts for three to five years. The remainder of the generation is then occupied with digesting the results of that spurt, modifying the new programs so that they will achieve great success and at the same time integrating them into the overall political framework. The end of the generation is marked by political acts that ratify and codify its accomplishments. By that time, there are already voices being heard calling for political responses to new challenges.

Belleville was founded at the very end of the sixth generation of American history, at the crossroads between the first generation under the Constitution and the generation that was to concentrate on the consolidation of the United States as a continental nation. Consequently, its pattern of challenge and response parallels that of the country as a whole to a remarkable extent, as indicated in Table 1 and in the following pages. Here, too, Belleville offers a good example of the pattern of the generations on the local plane.

The convergence of a new generation and the opening of a new frontier stage at the end of World War II make the postwar period examined here particularly important for understanding the influence of the generational progression on American politics. The impact of this generational progression in the history of Belleville is treated extensively in subsequent chapters.

The foregoing six theses with their corollaries are the themes of this book. The narrative sections in Chapters 2 through 5 represent an effort to work these themes out in a particular community and to view the interplay among them over the course of its history. The effort is not simply an idle exercise but, rather, an attempt to raise the discussion of community power to a new plane, one which takes into consideration a community's larger geo-historical setting, as well as its immediate political behavior, in assessing the system of power that makes it operative politically.

NOTES

1. For further elaboration of the civil community thesis, see Daniel J. Elazar, *Cities of the Prairie*, Introduction; and *Studying the Civil Community* (Philadelphia: Center for the Study of Federalism, 1970).

2. The frontier thesis sketched here is discussed in greater detail in *Cities of the Prairie*, Chapters 1 and 2.

3. For a more detailed discussion of the thesis presented here, see *Cities of the Prairie*, Part II and Appendix B.

4. See Daniel J. Elazar, *American Federalism: A View from the States* (New York: T. Y. Crowell, 1966), Chapters 4 and 5; and *Cities of the Prairie*, Parts 2 and 3.

5. Fuller delineation of the spheres and discussion of sectionalism in general can be found in *Cities of the Prairie*, Chapter 3.

6. See, in particular, Morton Grodzins, *The American System: A New View of Government in the United States*, edited by Daniel J. Elazar (Chicago: Rand McNally, 1966) and *American Federalism: A View from the States*.

7. Daniel J. Elazar, *Toward a Generational Theory of American Politics* (Philadelphia: Center for the Study of Federalism, 1970).

THE

SETTING

The Physical Basis of Belleville's Community

Belleville, the county seat of St. Clair County, is one of the six principal cities located in the Illinois section of the St. Louis metropolitan region.[1] The city of Belleville proper and those parts of its settled suburban fringe areas which were developed by or for Bellevillians together comprise the Belleville civil community (see Table 3).

Belleville, Illinois, lies about twenty miles southeast of St. Louis, on a long, narrow ridge of land that rises 25 to 150 feet above the surrounding countryside, a ridge that is part of the network of low bluffs forming the eastern rim of the Mississippi River Valley (see map, inside front cover). The major part of Belleville's settled area is on top of the ridge, which stretches southeastward from the beginning of the bluff line some twenty miles until it merges with the prairie plateau that is the heart of Illinois.

The settlement that is now the city of Belleville was founded in 1814 by order of the board of commissioners of St. Clair County. The county commissioners, who had come west from the "United States," wanted to establish a new city on the bluffs as the county seat, in an effort to move the center of county government out of French-dominated Cahokia, a much

TABLE 3

The Belleville Civil Community

St. Clair County

Federal Government Institutions   *State Offices in Belleville*
  United States Post Office   Drivers License Examining (Secretary of State)
  Scott Air Force Base   State Employment Service
                              Illinois Veterans Commission
                              Division of Services for Crippled Children
                                (University of Illinois)

Incorporated Municipalities
    City of Belleville
    City of O'Fallon
    Village of Swansea
    Village of Shiloh

School Districts   *Special Districts*
  Belleville High School   Park District
    and Junior College District   Sewage Districts
                                Fire Districts

Elementary School Districts   *Townships*
  District 118   Belleville
  Highmont   Canteen[a]
  Signal Hill   Caseyville[a]
  Harmony-Enge   Centerville[a]
  Belle-Valley   O'Fallon[a]
                              St. Clair[a]
                              Shiloh Valley[a]
                              Stookey[a]

Public Nongovernmental Bodies
    Chamber of Commerce
    Neighborhood Improvement
      Associations
    Civic and Service Organizations
    Volunteer Fire Departments

---

[a] Partially included in the civil community

older settlement on the Mississippi River. Thus the people who settled Belleville immediately adopted a hostile attitude toward the people living in the "American Bottoms" (as the area along the river is called), an attitude that has been reinforced in many ways since 1814 and remains an important factor in determining the course of civic life in the civil community.[2]

From the beginning, Belleville has grown in linear fashion on top of the ridge, along the main road that leads along the ridge from St. Louis southeastward via East St. Louis. Only in the area where that road is crossed by the original north-south road linking southern St. Clair County to Collinsville, Edwardsville, and settlements to the north has the urbanized area spread out into a more regular shape. Despite the influx of settlement into the area since World War II, the problem of providing water and sewer connections, or even proper drainage along the slopes of the ridge, has continued to confine the community's development to the ridge or to the bluffs immediately adjacent to it (see map, inside back cover). Consequently, the city is shaped socially and, to a degree, politically by its linear configuration, which reaches from the city limits of East St. Louis on the northwest and ends on the Illinois prairie to the southeast.

Belleville's general street plan follows the irregular pattern most commonly found in the South (see map, inside front cover). This in itself reflects the civil community's pattern of growth. The roads that gave the settlement its first configuration were laid out before the area was surveyed and divided into rectangular units by the federal land survey teams, and the lesser streets in Belleville opened since then have been fitted into this Southern-style road pattern. After the first structures were built near the intersection of the two main roads of pioneer days, other buildings were added piecemeal between the roads, without any effort to follow the geometric patterns found in most of the cities located on lands surveyed by the federal government in the greater West. The city's smaller streets are made even more irregular by the topography; many of them dead-end at the ridge line after a few blocks.

Neighborhoods, in the sense of residential areas distinguished by the quality and the character of the housing, are almost non-existent in Belleville. Indeed, such internal divisions as exist are clearly products of the fragmented and disjointed street plan that characterizes the city and that has itself been developed in response to the topography of the area. In place of neighborhoods, in the traditional sense, there are two relatively large, differentiated sections in the city, each composed of a series of "single-block" units.

The two principal sections recognized by most Bellevillians are (in local parlance) the East End and the West End. The West End consists of that area within and outside the city limits from the Belleville Township High School and Junior College campus westward to the East St. Louis city limits. It is the most recently settled of the sections and contains most of the migrants who have come to Belleville from East St. Louis since the end of World War II. The East End is old Belleville, a single section in the perceptions of the local residents, but divided by chronology of settlement into three subsections: original Belleville around the city's center; original West Belleville, west of Richland Creek and once an independent municipality; and "new" Belleville, that part of the East End within and outside the city limits, which was first settled in the 1920s and has filled up since World War II. The internal divisions within the East End have meaning only to the observer. Even the boundaries between the two sections are sufficiently indeterminate in the minds of the townspeople to make the foregoing imprecise description a better reflection of their local meaning than any effort at precise delimitation of their boundaries would do. The divisions had relatively little meaning in city politics from the time of the Civil War until recently, when the immigrants from East St. Louis became more numerous in the West End.

The importance of streets as the basis of social organization is nowhere better illustrated than in Belleville, where a street pattern which is abridged because of topography has prevented the unification of contiguously settled areas and has kept them separated into individual block units. The high proportion of dead-end and very short streets has prevented neighborhoods, in the accepted sense of the term, from coalescing, since there are limited possibilities for communication between blocks. In their place, homogeneous "blocks" have developed and stand out. Most of these blocks consist of residences opening onto short streets that lead off of the main St. Louis road and come to an end at the edge of the ridge. Under this system, quite frequently a block (that is, the two sides of a street) will have a similar pattern of architecture, and its occupants will share a similar social or economic background, while the next block will be different in both respects.

One semi-neighborhood exists in original Belleville in the area east of the Louisville and Nashville Railroad tracks, in the northeast part of the city. There, on a plateau-like area, the blocks are tied together by a complete system of roads where they do have the relatively homogeneous characteristics common to more traditional neighborhoods. This area was settled before the turn of the century by Southerners. Its architecture is predominantly rural and Southern, and it is likely that the people who came up from the South on the Louisville and Nashville Railroad settled right there.

It is possible that neighborhood awareness and cohesiveness may develop in the new subdivisions built in the 1950s and 1960s which cover areas large enough to take on a neighborhood identity. This possibly is reflected, in part, in the emergence of homeowners' associations which developed in some of these subdivisions to meet specific neighborhood needs in the early years of their settlement. However, even among the subdivisions where the topography does not demand it, many streets are being laid out in such a way as to maintain the old style of block-by-block patterns. This is particularly true in the new subdivisions of the East End in the southeast of the city, which are molded by "old Bellevillians" and where construction actually progresses on a block-by-block rather than subdivision basis. The West End subdivisions, on the other hand, taking their cue from East St. Louis, are being built to cover larger, contiguous territories, occasionally overcoming topographic barriers to do so.

On the basis of Belleville's most recent housing and subdivision developments, it can be concluded that the direct influence of topography on settlement patterns is diminishing. What is taking their place, however, is the artificial extension of settlement patterns which originally developed in response to those direct topographic influences, but which have now become rooted in the local culture into areas where they are no longer physically required. This is true on the expanding fringes of both sections of Belleville. Old line Bellevillians are extending their "ridge" patterns out onto the prairie, while old line East St. Louisians are extending their flatland patterns onto the ridge, with minimal modifications in both cases.

The Belleville experience with organizing the land for human settlement is typical—and significant. The tension between the "artificial" (in the sense of man-made) extension of what have become traditional patterns of settlement in Belleville into areas where the natural environment no longer demands them, and the inclination to alter the traditional patterns to take advantage of the different topographical base, is typical of the kind of tension between "society" and "nature" that is being generated on the metropolitan frontier today, in which "natural" patterns are substantially perpetuated through human culture, or "second nature." The homeowners' associations, on one hand, and subdivision control ordinances, on the other, become political manifestations of human effort to express and resolve this tension within the realm of action. They become necessary in inverse proportion to the decline of direct natural influences (which were once sufficient to maintain the latter) on previously devised cultural patterns.

Belleville also has a distinctive architecture of its own, with a style that is apparent even to the casual visitor. The city's architectural style originated after 1830, when large numbers of German immigrants began to settle in the civil community.

It represents a modification of the type of pointed-roof, stone structure found in parts of Germany, slightly altered for American conditions. This distinctive architecture is generally confined to the older sections of the city, where most of the city's original structures are still in use. The newer sections, particularly those built since World War II, reflect the more uniform patterns of contemporary American suburban architecture. Even so, some of the characteristics of the city's older architectural tradition have been incorporated into the newer homes, so that the impression remains that Belleville has a distinctive architectural pattern.

Belleville was originally settled by Southerners, and has continued to attract its share of the Southern migrants to the St. Louis area. Accordingly, in some of its neighborhoods, the buildings reflect Southern architectural styles of different periods.

Somewhat more important than sociological or architectural neighborhoods in the city are the city's seven wards and their precinct divisions—the "civil neighborhoods" of the civil community. While these civil neighborhoods are not recognized by many people other than those directly involved in local politics, it may fairly be said that their organization for political purposes represents the highest level of neighborhood organization in the civil community. The wards and precincts in the city of Belleville proper were redistricted in 1960 in response to the changes brought on by the postwar population shifts, which altered many of the old patterns. The redistricting was accomplished with relatively little struggle, an indication that even in regard to political organization, neighborhood identities in Belleville are weak.

The precincts are considerably more important than the wards in the larger scheme of local politics, for two reasons. In the first place, the topography and the block-by-block separation favor precinct organization as being more rationally suited to the socio-physical pattern of settlement, particularly in the city. Even more significant, the wards have meaning only in city elections, while the precincts are also important in county politics. Political party organization in St. Clair County, as in the rest of Illinois, is based on the precinct committeemen who are voting members of the county central committees of their respective parties. In a county as tightly organized politically as St. Clair County, control of the precinct offices is necessary for control of the county political organization of either party, while control of the precincts is necessary to win elections. Accordingly, the precinct committeeman has a crucial role to play in city, township, county, state, and national elections, which makes his geographic unit of political organization very valuable to those interested in politics.

TABLE 4

Nativity and Migration in the City of Belleville, 1960

Nativity	
Percent foreign-born	2.3
Percent native of foreign/mixed parentage	11.0
Total foreign stock	13.3
Leading country of origin as percent of foreign stock	46.0 (Germany)
Migration	
Residents in same house since 1955	51.1%
Arrivals from different county since 1955	15.0

Source: U.S. Census Bureau Data

The Socio-Religious Basis of Belleville's Politics

The cultural base underlying contemporary Belleville politics is a product of the several migrational streams and currents which contributed people to the civil community. These cultural streams have of course been modified by the passage of time and by events in Belleville since their arrival. Today their legacy is most clearly manifested in the socio-religious alignments within the civil community, which remain of great importance. These alignments substantially reflect the origins of their "members" in the currents of settlers who came into the Belleville civil community from other parts of the nation and the world and who impressed their socio-cultural patterns upon the community in its early days, thus providing the basis from which the community could develop its own internal amalgam of these patterns.

Cultural divisions with ethnic overtones were reflected in the pattern of religious affiliations from the first days of the settlement of Belleville. Some sense of these divisions can be gained from a review of the history of institutionalized religion in the civil community. In delineating the religious institutionalization of these cultural divisions, it should be understood that there is no perfect correlation between the particular "churches" and the cultural streams. Individuals born into one stream may choose to become "galvanized" into another, a feat often accomplished through church membership. Even more important, patterns of religious affiliation for a whole community may be altered by some "accidental" event, such as a major religious revival that strengthens a new denomination at the expense of older ones. Nevertheless, the correlation between cultural stream and religious denomination appears high and is useful as an indicator (albeit imperfect) of the cultural composition of the local community.

Since the Southerners were the first to arrive in the Belleville area, their currents provided the first underpinning for the development of local cultural patterns. The oldest religious groups in the community are the Southern Protestant denominations which reflect the cultural patterns making up the Southern stream. Even though religious services were held earlier, the particular character of Southern individualism did not encourage the formation of an institutionalized church until 1831, when a Baptist congregation was founded, primarily by Southerners.

In 1832 the settlers of English origin in the community organized a second church, the English Methodist Church. Though the church had obvious ethnic overtones, it also appears to have served as the representative institution for those settlers who shared the culture of Americans who had come from the Middle States. The organization of a third church completed the religious institutionalization of the three major subcultures in the United States. The Yankees, a minority group in the community from the beginning, founded the Presbyterian Church, which began holding services in 1833 and was formally organized in 1839. Within its ranks could be found most of the local Yankee element and those sympathetic to the Yankee subculture, which differed much more sharply from that of the Southerners than did the Middle States subculture.

By the time the churches were becoming formally organized, the first wave of European immigrants had reached Belleville. These were the Germans, mostly from southern Germany, who were divided about equally between Protestantism and Catholicism in their socio-religious backgrounds and whose religious and cultural differences could be traced back at least to the Reformation. Whatever the bonds of "nationality" between them, these two elements actually represented two different cultural currents.

The two elements organized separately from the first, just as the Americans had done. In 1835 the first German Protestant congregation held services. The congregation was formally organized as the Evangelical Church in 1839. In 1836 the German Catholics founded their first church. Twelve years later they founded their first parochial school at the same time the German Protestants were organizing what was to become the Belleville public school system. Since then, the two systems have grown side by side.

Since the coming of the Germans the Catholic population of the Belleville civil community has grown with the Protestant population quite steadily. In 1961 the civil community's population was about equally divided between the two religious groups. Belleville became the seat of a Catholic diocese in 1887, and is considered a minor center of the Catholic Church in the United States.

The Jews, while strongly identified with the immigrants from northern Europe, form a cultural stream of their own. Some Jews came to Belleville at the time of the German immigration and descendants of those early families remain in the community. However, there was not a sufficient number of Jewish settlers to organize a synagogue until 1919. Today the Jews remain a very small, though active, minority in the community.

The last group to organize along formal congregational lines in the community was the Fundamentalist Protestant element, which developed its own institutionalized churches only in this century. As the older Protestant churches became more "respectable" and religiously "liberal" in their orientation, important social and religious differences began to set them apart from simple believers, most of whom were on a lower socioeconomic level. The local, predominantly Southern-originated Fundamentalists found themselves with no place to go. As their strength was augmented by new immigrants (generally from the South) who had no ties to local churches, they began to organize their own institutions. The largest and most important Fundamentalist churches are the Full Gospel Church, organized in 1936, and the Pentecostal Church, organized in 1942. In addition, there are many other smaller churches which fall into this category.[3]

The religious cleavage in the Belleville civil community, while generally quite benign, is the most pronounced of all the intracommunity cleavages. For most civic purposes Belleville is implicitly divided into four parts: two major "recognized" and dominant religious subcommunities (Protestant and Catholic), a third very small recognized subcommunity (Jewish) and an emergent fourth subcommunity (Fundamentalist) whose identity is not yet clear and whose public recognition as a distinct element in local civic affairs is virtually nil. The major element in this cleavage, the Protestant-Catholic balance, is nearly always in the public eye.

What is distinctive about the religious cleavage in Belleville is that it is a subcommunal division within an integrated community. The community is delineated along socio-religious lines but is not divided into hostile camps along those lines. The existence of these subcommunities is assumed as part of the very structure of the overall community. They are not isolated ghettoizing factors but loosely structured mechanisms for community action. Consequently there is a great deal of cooperation among all segments of the community despite the general awareness of these divisions.

The existence of continuing subcommunities with permanent institutions of their own does not mean that people do not relate to one another as individuals across socio-religious lines or that, for some people, other interests (politics, for example) do not become more important as unifying forces than the socio-religious one. Belleville's socio-religious communalism is, in the last analysis, an American phenomenon, not some version of the Near Eastern Millet system. Every individual has the very real (if subtly limited) right to choose whether to participate in it or not, and to determine how he wishes to participate. He is not forced to depend on his ties with a particular subcommunity in order to function as a member of the larger community, even though the extent of his effectiveness in some fields of community endeavor may depend on the character of his relationship with his religious subcommunity.

The socio-religious facet of the local power structure is built on twin Protestant and Catholic bases, with the addition of a quasi-independent Jewish base. The first two bases are structured internally in a roughly hierarchial manner. Delineation of the hierarchy of influence within each of the subcommunities and the relationship between them requires some oversimplification, but in general it is a useful means of delineating an important facet of the structure of local political power.

Within the Protestant subcommunity the most prestigious religious institution is the First Presbyterian Church. In the tradition of its Yankee founders, whose culture placed great emphasis on community service, its members make an effort to lead the community in civic and artistic endeavors. This effort is consciously acknowledged by them, at least within the confines of their church. A large number of the Protestants among the downtown businessmen (the leading business element) are members of this church. Several local politicians are reputed to have joined in order to benefit from association with First Presbyterian. Since the Protestants were the original holders of power in Belleville and have conceded only a share, albeit a roughly equal share, of power to the Catholics, the First Presbyterian Church may be the single most important socio-religious institution in the civil community, perhaps more for its function as a determinant of who associates socially with whom than for any other purpose. The minister of that church is traditionally the most powerful Protestant minister in town, though, of course, the Catholic bishop who heads the diocese is probably the most important clergyman, backed as he is by the power of a more tightly organized church.

On a social par with the Presbyterians are the local affiliates of the United Church of Christ. Mostly Evangelical and Reformed churches established by Germans, the local UCC also includes two churches which were Congregationalist before the merger of the two church groups. A number of their members are politically influential as individuals, although the churches themselves have no local reputation for political leadership. Most of the Protestant leadership that does not come from the Presbyterian Church comes from the old Evangelical and Reformed churches. As in the case of the former, community activity and service are long-standing traditions among those elements that established the churches of this denomination.

Below these two denominations, slightly separated in terms of status, are the Lutherans. Their national and local position, slightly outside of the "mainstream" of institutionalized American Protantism, is made apparent, in part, by their sponsorship of a parochial school whose existence seems clearly designed to fill the gap in Christian education created by the

Presbyterian-Evangelical domination of the otherwise secularly oriented public schools. The Lutheran Church has a long tradition of isolation from politics. The bulk of its local congregations reflect this in their members' minimal involvement in active public service. This tradition has never precluded individual Lutherans from assuming important public roles in Belleville on the basis of their personal interests.

As the two broad-based Protestant denominations, the Methodist and Baptist Churches generally share the same status and influence level. Their congregations generally occupy the community's great middle ground. Politically this means that these churches probably supply a large number of precinct and civic workers but relatively few people in the upper levels of influence. With no particular church tradition of community involvement, individual Methodists and Baptists may choose to be active in public affairs on the basis of personal interest alone. Those who do become active find no barriers to becoming influential provided they have the requisite talents or connections. Some of the Baptist congregations, particularly those of Southern origin, are really much closer in socio-economic position to the Fundamentalists and should be considered in the same category.

Far below the foregoing groups in status and influence are the Fundamentalists who are by and large excluded from major participation in the community. This exclusion is partly by choice. The Fundamentalists generally occupy the lower socio-economic positions in the community. Politically they range from apathetic to alienated. Their churches are dedicated to individual salvation, not communal redemption, which suits them well. In Belleville, as in American society as a whole, the Fundamentalists include the otherwise excluded groups. Their exclusion is so universal and reflects such basic differences in values and attitudes that the Fundamentalists are apparently emerging as a subcommunity in their own right. This is reflected nationally in the division between the liberal and conservative Protestant churches. Locally the Fundamentalists have yet to challenge the political status quo (or even to show an interest in doing so) in order to gain representation in the day-to-day decision-making councils of the community. This is due at least partly to the substantially apolitical nature of their membership. Their influence is occasionally felt at the polls in conflicts over community issues, where they are stirred as individuals, but nowhere else.

Among the Catholics the hierarchial arrangement of the individual parish churches is more difficult to determine. Generally, the most influential Catholics group themselves around the diocesan offices. At any given time they can be identified individually. The Catholics are a highly structured and organized subcommunity, with their own credit unions, insurance companies, youth centers, and hospital, all of which have been stimulated by the diocese as a matter of policy. This fact frequently bothers the Protestants, since they feel that the Catholics can mobilize more power at times when they feel they must be heard than can the loosely joined Protestant subcommunity. The bishops, however, have been careful not to intervene openly in local politics.

Occasionally the latent Protestant-Catholic rivalry comes to the surface on a specific issue. The maintenance of hospitals in American society has become a function of the religious subcommunities and in the process has acquired certain religious overtones. In Belleville, when the Catholics built St. Elizabeth's Hospital, the top Protestant leadership reacted by establishing Memorial Hospital, which continues to be supported by Protestant funds. This was not altogether pleasing to many of the Protestants in the community who felt that one hospital was enough and that this type of competition was not necessary. Memorial Hospital has never become the equal of St. Elizabeth's, but it continues to exist and is maintained now if only as a matter of "face."

The Jews, who are closer to the Protestants than to the Catholics, sometimes appear politically to be a wing of the Protestant subcommunity. The minuscule number of Jews in the community (perhaps one hundred families) prevents their having a well-defined internal structure, particularly since they are well integrated into the larger community. At any given time, however, one can point to one or two downtown business leaders who are implicitly recognized as representing the Jewish subcommunity in community decision-making.

By and large the leaders from the socio-religious groups are not the professional religionists. The clergy, as such, play a very small role in community life other than the role dictated by their ministries. Even the Catholic clergy are careful to confine their visible activities to their churches. The leadership of the three subcommunities in civic affairs is almost exclusively a lay leadership. Furthermore, although its existence is recognized implicitly in community affairs, it is a very loosely structured leadership with no formal mandate in any sense of the term.

Aside from the hospital issue and occasional issues like it, there has been little overt cleavage between the socio-religious subcommunities. There is none over the liquor issue, as there is between the socio-religious groups in other civil communities where Protestants have a "dry" tradition and Catholics are traditionally "wet," because German-influenced Belleville is a "tolerant" community (meaning that members of both communities have always done some drinking and that the amount of prohibitionist sentiment in the community is negligible). A potential issue is the extensive property holding of the Catholic Church. Many Protestants are uneasy about an increase in the power of the Catholic Church as a result of its continuing to acquire real property. Steps are quietly taken on occasion by Protestant businessmen to prevent acquisition of additional property by the Catholic Church. While discussed privately, this issue had not come out into the open in the early 1960s.

In 1960 Belleville had virtually no Negroes. There were fewer than two hundred in the civil community, nearly all of them apparently descended from long-time resident families, some of which may have been in the area since the days when *de facto* slavery existed locally. The Negroes in Belleville had always lived very quietly and "knew their place," which meant that they filled the most menial jobs and did not attempt to participate in politics or civic affairs. White Bellevillians have made every effort to restrict the number of Negro settlers and to keep their influence nil. Indeed, the Negro population has varied little since 1870, actually having reached its high point in 1890. (Table 5)

TABLE 5

Afro-American Population in Belleville, 1840-1960

1840	(59 slaves)	1900	230
1850	. . .	1910	216
1860	85	1920	180
1870	157	1930	178
1880	236	1940	154
1890	241	1950	196
		1960	195

Source: U.S. Census Bureau Data

The Economic Basis of Belleville's Independence

By good fortune, Belleville was located in a relatively favorable position for the development of an economy based on exploitation of raw materials. There are large deposits of bituminous coal just east of the city, and coal-mining activities (substantially diminished since the 1950s) date back to the mid-nineteenth century. High-grade limestone is also found in the area. It was used extensively in the construction of the first houses and business edifices. Clay, molding and building sand, coke and natural gas are also available for extraction in the vicinity of Belleville. Furthermore, Belleville's proximity to the Mississippi River with its system of waterways makes it possible to import other raw materials and to export manufactured products with relative ease.

Thus it is not surprising that Belleville has been a center of small industry since its beginnings as a community. The first local industry actually antedates the founding of the settlement. Several mills were established in 1810 within what are today the city's limits to provide milling services for the farmers settling in the Belleville area. The first manufacturing industry, a distillery, was established in 1820 to take advantage of the local corn surplus. It existed for ten years and gave way to several German-founded breweries, the first of which was established in 1832. One of those breweries is the Carling Brewing Company, today a leading local industry.

The change from the distilling to the brewing industry was symptomatic of the change in the community's composition. Until 1830 Southerners formed the majority of the settlers in the Belleville area, and their favorite alcoholic beverage was bourbon whiskey. After 1830 the Germans came to the area in large numbers. They were beer drinkers and brought with them from the "old country" the art of brewing beer (specifically the process of "lagering"). As they became the dominant element in the community, beer-drinking replaced the consumption of whiskey as the primary form of indulgence and was supported accordingly.

In 1825 coal mining began east of the city. It reached its peak in the late nineteenth century and has since declined in importance in the face of competition from other fuels. The development of automated methods for the extraction of coal has contributed further to the decline in importance of the industry as a source of employment, although mining still plays a role in the economy of the Belleville area.

In 1840 a cigar industry was founded locally, again by Germans who brought the art with them from their old country homes. This industry contributed to the development of a skilled, pro-union labor force which made Belleville one of the pioneer "union towns" in the United States. This industry has since disappeared, a victim of competition from other sections of the country.

Agricultural implements were manufactured for a time in Belleville after 1847, but as the industry passed from its early entrepreneurial stage into the corporate mass production era it became centralized in northern Illinois communities. Belleville's plant suffered the fate of most of the small pioneer companies in the agricultural implement line: it was absorbed by one of its more successful rivals and was closed down.

The outcome of the struggle for industrial development in the pre-Civil War period determined the upper limits of Belleville's growth in that period. Just off the mainstream of American economic development, Belleville was able to capitalize on its location and natural resources sufficiently to sustain a rate of growth that was not far out of line from that of similar cities in Illinois, but it was not in a sufficiently strong economic position to become a pacesetter in its state or region. It was as if Belleville's position as a medium-sized city was already determined by its sectional position.

The civil community's major industrial growth came after 1870, at the same time as that of the rest of the St. Louis metropolitan region. Unlike its sister cities in the American Bottoms, however, Belleville's industrial development was not so much an extension of St. Louis interests into Illinois as it was a product of local initiative. In 1873 the first of several foundries was established in Belleville. The number of foundries grew after 1875, and the foundry industry has continued to play an important part in the community's industrial development. During the 1880s the foundries, particularly the nail mills which supplied parts and nails for the settlement of the prairies to the west of the St. Louis metropolitan region, triggered a large industrial boom in the Belleville area. Most of the present industries in the community had their origins in this period, which coincided with the extension of the urban-industrial frontier into the medium-sized communities of the greater West.

The boom of the 1880s and 1890s gave Belleville a highly diversified industrial base which has continued to flourish without succumbing to the nationwide trend toward industrial concentration and giantism. Much of Belleville's industry remains home-owned. In 1961 the Belleville civil community manufactured stoves, shoes, stencil machines, tacks, garments, machine tool patterns and dies, boilers, industrial furnaces, dresses, bricks, tile cutters, trousers, and corrugated paper boxes. Bellevillians mined three million tons of coal annually, brewed beer, and milled flour. The largest civilian employer was the Carling Brewing Company.

Continued local ownership of Belleville's industrial base has enhanced the social and economic stability of the civil community. The combination of local ownership and industrial diversification has strengthened local civic and political life by insuring that those who control a major share of the economic destiny of the community are themselves tied to the same destiny. At the same time, no single individual or concern can become so powerful economically as to prevent broad popular local control. Local economic leaders are potential civic leaders by virtue of their local commitments, but they are not encouraged to become local dictators by virtue of their economic power.

The largest employer in the Belleville area in 1960 was Scott Air Force Base, a military installation established in 1917. The base's impact on the local economy is considerable and its proper support is a matter of no little concern to the local leadership. The existence of the base has had political ramifications as well, in terms of both intralocal relationships within the Belleville civil community and Belleville's interests as a community on the national scene.

Belleville's transportation facilities have been linked to the larger metropolitan transportation network around St. Louis at least since the 1840s. It is likely that Belleville was profoundly affected as early as the 1820s by its location close to St. Louis. Its original connections with the outside world were by stagecoach via the St. Louis Road (then, as now, the city's main thoroughfare). The coach line maintained regular service with the support of a mail subsidy from the federal government, which, at least in its early years, made it possible for service to be provided at a profit. While this service brought Belleville within St. Louis' commercial orbit, the time required to cover the distance limited the possibilities for commuting in any form.

After 1830 the major roads leading into the Belleville area were built by private companies and maintained as toll roads, some as late as 1917. The St. Louis Road, the most important of them all, was not taken over by public authorities until the first decade of the twentieth century, remaining a toll road, and a plank road at that, until the "good roads" movement led to its rebuilding. This continued hegemony of private enterprise in a field which even then had long been recognized as a public obligation in most parts of the country is indicative of a persisting attitude among most politically articulate Bellevillians that government activity should be strictly limited and expanded only for the most serious causes.

The first railroad did not reach Belleville until fairly late. The main line of the Louisville and Nashville Railroad was built through the city in 1870 in time to help stimulate the industrial boom of the 1870s and the following decade. The Southern Railway came in with its main line shortly thereafter, and subsequently a branch of the Illinois Central was built into the city. This convergence of railroads was of great importance in stimulating Belleville's growth in the last quarter of the nineteenth century. Belleville's position on two main lines that connected St. Louis to the southeast affected its patterns of settlement and of production since it was easy for its industries to export to the southeast, which provided a ready market for much of what it makes, while at the same time people from the southeast could come into Belleville to settle with relative ease. The coming of the railroad also put Belleville within an hour's ride of St. Louis, making it possible for some Bellevillians to work and shop in the larger metropolis.

Belleville has access to the water facilities of St. Louis and the Mississippi waterway system. It also uses the air facilities of St. Louis and advertises (with some exaggeration) that it is only half an hour from the St. Louis airport.[4] Those Bellevillians interested in promoting economic development are presently active in the promotion of a nine-foot channel on the Kaskaskia River to New Athens. New Athens, only fourteen miles southeast of Belleville, could well become its "Piraeus" and eliminate some of the disadvantages of Belleville's present "high and dry" position.

With the advent of modern highways in the 1920s, Belleville's ties to the St. Louis transportation network were increased, making it possible to commute into the latter city with little difficulty. The most important recent addition to this transportation system is State Highway 460, a divided, four-lane, limited-access highway that connects Belleville with East St. Louis and places it within twenty minutes of downtown St. Louis. During the 1950s improvements were also made on roads connecting Belleville to its sister cities in the Madison-St. Clair County area, particularly to Collinsville and Edwardsville, which have eliminated some of the long-prevalent necessity for all traffic to flow into St. Louis or East St. Louis before going to other parts of the metropolitan region.

Belleville has three banks and five savings and loan associations. The oldest bank was established in 1859 as the Belleville Savings Bank. In the 1950s it was absorbed by the Belleville National Bank, a relative upstart, founded in 1928. The oldest bank still operating under the same name is the First National Bank established in 1874. It is also the most important of the three banks. The St. Clair National Bank was established in 1919. In 1961 the three banks had an aggregate $70 million in deposits.

In the period since World War II the five savings and loan associations have had the most spectacular record of growth among the civil community's financial institutions. By 1961 they had a combined total of $60 million in deposits, which represented an increase of over 50 percent since the late 1940s. This great increase has brought them into a position rivaling that of the banks as sources of credit in the community. As such, they have become forces to be reckoned with in local politics, increasing the diffusion of power locally by altering the balance of power (which had traditionally rested with the banks) within the downtown business subcommunity.[5]

Belleville's labor force consists primarily of skilled or at least semi-skilled workers of a much higher quality than in the rest of the metropolitan area. The 1960 census showed that approximately 25 percent of the employed in the civil community were engaged in industry, another 25 percent in commerce, about 12½ percent in agriculture, 25 percent in government, while approximately 12½ percent were unemployed.

This extraordinarily high unemployment figure reflected, in the main, the unemployment generated by the closing or automating of the coal mines in the area and elimination of jobs in the mines. Because most of the miners whose jobs were eliminated were over the age at which they could reasonably hope to find other employment and because they lacked the necessary skills, they have remained on the list of the unemployed. The high figure for 1960 was reduced somewhat in the following years as the country as a whole emerged from the recession of the late 1950s. As a community, Belleville has been singularly unconcerned about this high rate of unemployment, although it is making a considerable effort to attract new industry to meet the general need for economic development.

The working men of Belleville are highly unionized. There are fifty-three unions in the city, almost as many as there are manufacturing firms (fifty-four). Most are old craft unions affiliated with the American Federation of Labor before the AFL-CIO merger. In 1951 the local AFL council listed a membership of 10,000 out of a total population in the civil community of perhaps 50,000. The very diversity of industry in the community has encouraged this proliferation of independent unions. Most of the unions are small locals containing highly specialized craftsmen and reflecting the great diversity of industrial production in the Belleville community.

Unions have been active in Belleville since before the Civil War. They were brought by many of the same Germans who brought with them libraries and public schools as reflections of the middle-class concerns of skilled craftsmen rather than as militant organizations for a class-conscious proletariat. They have been well accepted as integral parts of the civil community, at least since the post-Civil War period. As early as 1891 a general citywide labor union existed, and the Central Trades and Labor Council remains a powerful force in the community today. Indeed, as will be shown later, the labor movement is one of the three pillars of the multicentered oligarchy that governs the Belleville civil community.

Since the end of World War II a new element has appeared on the local economic scene — the commuters. This element includes workers, professionals, and businessmen who earn their living in St. Louis or in the East St. Louis area while living in the Belleville civil community. Its most striking feature is the virtually total exclusion of these people from active politics in Belleville. Some of the commuters—particularly those from St. Louis who find Belleville a good place to live because, as they put it, "We drive to and from work with the sun at our backs instead of in our eyes"—have yet to develop ties to Illinois and Illinois politics. Others, particularly those economically tied to East St. Louis, retain their political ties to that community as well. Whatever minor impact the commuters have made on local politics stems from the latter group, some of whom have attempted to enter precinct politics to strengthen their positions of political influence at the county level.

In sum, the heart of Belleville's economic base consists of a group of small, highly diversified industries mostly owned locally, most of which date back to the industrial boom of the late nineteenth century when Belleville was assimilated into the urban-industrial frontier. These locally owned industries are served by a skilled labor force highly organized into a large number of craft unions. Superimposed on this industrial base are two twentieth-century-style economic institutions—Scott

Air Force Base with its large civilian payroll, and the growing
number of residents who commute to work in the St. Louis-
East St. Louis area—whose full effect on the civil community is
yet to be felt.

The striking aspect of Belleville's industrial base is its continued, close approximation of the nineteenth-century liberal,
capitalistic model, based on locally owned small-scale industry,
which has maintained direct employer-employee relationships
and which demands a high level of skilled workmanship. The
social structure of "old Belleville" reflects the middle-class
characteristics supported and encouraged by such an industrial
base. Of the wage earners in the community, 85 percent are
homeowners (see Table 6). The rise of the two new-style economic institutions, however, has brought a new population into
the civil community, one which shows signs of differing substantially from the "old Bellevillians." This population is not
yet politically articulate in the civil community. What will
happen when it becomes politically articulate is difficult to
foresee.

TABLE 6

Home Ownership in Belleville, 1940-1960

	1940	1950	1960
Owner-occupied	4,662	6,577	8,738
Renter-occupied	3,901	3,845	3,340

Source: U.S. Census, Characteristics of the Population, 1940, 1950, 1960.

NOTES

1. The City of St. Louis and St. Louis County in Missouri, plus Madison and St. Clair Counties in Illinois, are combined by the United States
Census Bureau into a single, Standard Metropolitan Statistical Area
(SMSA). The size, interstate character, and governmental complexity
of this SMSA are such, however, that this writer believes them to be
more accurately described as a metropolitan region centering on St.

Louis in certain ways, but generally separated into two metropolitan areas by the Mississippi River.

2. The sources from which the historical materials for this book were taken are listed in Appendix B.

3. All references to the fundamentalists here refer to those who are members of organized fundamentalist churches, or who participate in groups or families united around such churches. There are, of course, many theological fundamentalists in the other churches as well, but they are not distinguishable as a socio-economic group in the same way.

4. A more reasonable estimate would be closer to an hour or even an hour and a half in driving time.

5. The growth of the savings and loan associations in Belleville appears to be a manifestation of a national phenomenon. According to the 1962 *Savings and Loan Fact Book* of the United States Savings and Loan League, in 1945 the nation's savings and loan associations held $7.4 billion in savings, as compared to the commercial banks' holdings of $29.9 billion. In 1961 the former held $70.9 billion and the latter $74.8 billion.

CHAPTER THREE

THE
CONSTITUTION
OF THE
CIVIL COMMUNITY

The Limits of the Civil Community

The Belleville civil community consists of much more than the area embraced by the Belleville municipality. While the civil community's geographic limits are vague, it can be delimited according to the patterns of communication linking the governments and public nongovernmental institutions which serve it. The nucleus of the Belleville civil community today, as before, is clearly the city of Belleville, but the civil community itself has for many years extended beyond the city's boundaries in one way or another (see Table 7).[1]

Even in the nineteenth century East Belleville and West Belleville, although incorporated as separate cities, were part of the same civil community, tied together from the first by the school district that has always embraced both. While consolidation of the two cities temporarily restored the juxtaposition of municipal boundaries with those of the civil community soon thereafter, the settlement limits of West Belleville were again extended beyond the city limits. Additional newcomers settled to the west of old West Belleville in what is now called the West End, which became part of the civil community even when it still had not been incorporated into the city. Part of the West End was finally annexed to the city in 1906, less to

TABLE 7

A Statistical Profile of the Belleville Civil Community

I. The City of Belleville: Basic Data

Population (1960)		37,264
Area (1960)		8.5 square miles

Education (1960)

persons 25 and over
median school years completed		9.8 years
completed less than 5 years		4.5%
completed high school or more		34.6%

persons 5-24 years enrolled in school
total		8,418
private schools through elementary level		37.4%

Number of families (1960)		10,104

Income
aggregate (1959 of 1960 pop.)		$82,000,000
median income (1959 of families)		$6,440
under $3,000		13.0%
$10,000 and over		17.3%

Employment (1960)
total		14,021
manufacturing		27.4%
retail and wholesale trade		19.5%
white collar occupations		49.8%

Manufacturing firms
total		67
with 20 or more employees	(1963)	24
	(1958)	28
value added by manufacture	(1963)	$30,924,000
	(1959)	$28,421,000

Retail trade
establishments	(1963)	517
	(1958)	535
sales	(1963)	$77,745,000
	(1958)	$63,917,000

TABLE 7 Continued

Wholesale trade

establishments	(1963)	68
	(1958)	NA
sales	(1963)	$19,861,000
	(1958)	——

City Government Finances (1964–65)

general revenue

total	$2,857,000
intergovernmental	417,000

taxes

total	$1,720,000
property	$1,165,000

general expenditure

total	$2,341,000
highways	519,000
health and welfare	7,000
police protection	257,000
fire protection	262,000
sewage	662,000
sanitation other than sewage	132,000
parks and recreation	139,000
debt outstanding	4,504,000

City government employees	229
City payroll	$94,000

II. Population Growth in the Civil Community

Census[a]	1930	1940	1950	1960
Belleville	28,425	28,405	32,721	37,264
St. Clair Twp.	3,956	3,783	7,374	13,831
Stookey Twp.	962	1,381	2,229	6,725
Shiloh Valley Twp.	1,291	2,145	9,899[b]	3,385[b]
Caseyville Twp.	2,929	4,094	7,822	16,872
(excluding Caseyville)	2,186	3,229	6,613	14,537
Totals[c]	36,820	38,943	58,836	80,742

	Belleville	Swansea	St. Clair Twp.	Stookey Twp.
1960	37,264	3,018	13,831	6,725
1950	32,721	1,816	7,374	2,229
Gain	4,543	1,202	6,457	4,496
	13.9%	66.2%	87.6%	201.7%

TABLE 7 Continued

	Caseyville Twp. (excluding Caseyville Village)		Caseyville Twp.
1960	14,537		16,872
1950	6,613		7,822
Gain	7,924		9,050
	119.8%		115.7%
	Shiloh Valley Twp.		Belleville Metropolitan Area
1950	9,899	1960	80,742
1960	8,385	1950	58,836
Loss	1,514	Gain	21,906
	15.3%		37.2%

a Official U.S. Census, as analyzed by the Chamber of Commerce, Belleville, Illinois.

b Includes Scott Air Force Base.

c Excludes that part of the Village of Caseyville Township, and does not include that area of Canteen Township lying on both sides of the most westerly city limits.

acquire the population that lived there than to obtain the connection necessary to bring Belleville within the range of the waterworks that provided the Illinois shore with water from the Mississippi River. Although the area of settlement was more extensive, the original annexation in 1906 was confined to the St. Louis road and a narrow strip on either side of it. Fifty years passed before the areas to the north and south of the road were added to the city, long after they had otherwise been absorbed into the civil community.

The pattern of growth and absorption in the civil community has remained relatively stable from the mid-nineteenth century to the present. The city of Belleville has remained the center of the civil community, growing in size with the whole community, but never quite including all of it. Belleville was and is the focus of government, but three other incorporated municipalities serve segments of the civil community. The village of Swansea is located just to the north of downtown Belleville, tucked into the city's side. It was incorporated in 1895 apparently to insure a predominantly rural environment for its residents, who, while spending their money and educating their children in Belleville, did not wish to encourage the denser urban development which was the tendency in Belleville proper.

The city of O'Fallon and the village of Shiloh to the east of Belleville are related to it in something of an exurban way. O'Fallon is an old community, incorporated in 1865, which has been absorbed into the Belleville civil community with the growth of automobile transportation. Shiloh is somewhat younger as an entity, incorporated in 1905. It shares an elementary school with O'Fallon and, like the latter, has been absorbed into the larger civil community as a residential area for automobile commuters. Although Swansea, O'Fallon, and Shiloh have independent municipal governments which provide minimal services, they remain tributaries of the city of Belleville in most respects. All three are also included in the Belleville Township High School and Junior College District.

The four municipalities are located in all or part of eight townships, adding greatly to the considerable confusion of political boundaries which is characteristic of the Madison-St. Clair area. The city of Belleville proper is coterminous with the Township of the City of Belleville—what is known as a "city township" in Illinois. It remains an independent governmental unit that performs the functions for which townships are responsible in the state for the same territory as the city government, surviving as a source of jobs for the professional politicians. On the northwest the civil community extends slightly into Centerville and Canteen Townships, neither of which is politically part of the bundle of governments that make up the Belleville civil community. Caseyville Township is partly within the limits of the civil community, as defined by such local agencies as the Chamber of Commerce, but by common consent, the village of Caseyville is not. St. Clair and Stookey Townships encompass the major incorporated segments of the civil community, virtually surrounding the city of Belleville, except at the far northwest corner. Politically, both are within the civil community. O'Fallon and Shiloh Valley Townships, which include the two municipalities of the same name to the east of Belleville, are included as the exurban extension of the civil community.

The third set of governments in the civil community includes the school governments. Central to all of them is the Belleville Township High School and Junior College District, created in 1916 as a high school district and expanded to include the junior college in 1946. The special state charter which created the district is a document that strongly reinforces the idea of civil community as it is outlined in this book, by giving the high school and junior college special communitywide status, even while many elementary school districts exist within it to service the civil community's various subdivisions. If it is possible to give the civil community formal boundaries, the boundaries of the high school and junior college district are the most appropriate.

Actually only two-thirds of the secondary school students in the Belleville civil community attend the public high school. The other third are enrolled in the Catholic high school. Still, it is the public institution which serves as a center for the entire community. Aside from their primary mission to provide education for the community's youth, the major contribution of the high school and junior college to the life of the community is their combined service as the center of the community's aesthetic, cultural, and intellectual activities. In this respect, their plays, exhibits, band and orchestra concerts, and in a fundamental sense, their physical facilities, which are used by other groups not affiliated with the school for any number of purposes, from the concerts of the Belleville Philharmonic Society to the local veterans' organizations, offer the advantages of a small cultural center. Since Belleville's civic leaders support an extensive cultural program, this is a meaningful service which also contributes to unifying the civil community.

The high school and junior college enable those living in the civil community to identify themselves with Belleville in many ways, especially through the high school football and basketball teams, which serve as a unifying force in the civil community to an extent that is often not appreciated by those in larger urban communities. Even better for the downtown business-men, the students and their parents are drawn in to do much of their shopping in Belleville. Belleville is also the center of such urban cultural and recreational activities in which the students and their parents participate.

In addition to the high school and junior college district, the Belleville civil community is served by six common school dis-tricts. The largest is District 118, which includes most of the city of Belleville proper, part of Swansea, and some of the sur-rounding unincorporated territory. It includes eight elementary schools and two junior high schools. In addition to this central district there are five very small districts, each with only one school, which have resisted consolidation in a desire to preserve neighborhood control of elementary education. Among them is the Highmont District at the far reaches of the West End, the Harmony-Enge District which consisted of two schools until their amalgamation into one in 1962, the Belle Valley Dis-trict in the East End, and the Whiteside District. These districts have jealously maintained their independence, keeping their single schools as symbols of neighborhood unity while sending their children to the Belleville Township High School and Junior College. At least in the Signal Hill District, this reflects the existence of a socio-economic cleavage; there a local "upper crust" is striving to maintain a separate neighborhood school for their children that will remain under their own control.

Despite the multiplicity of public school districts some 50 percent of the elementary school children in the Belleville civil community attend parochial schools. All but one of the schools are Catholic, the first of them established at the same time as the public schools to provide a non-Protestant education for the

Catholic youth of the community. The other is a Lutheran school of much more recent vintage.

There are also several special districts serving the Belleville civil community. One is the Belleville Park District, a virtually nonfunctioning government which maintains two parks, both established in the 1920s, and does little else. It has very little support in the community. Whatever additional park and recreation activities have been undertaken in the Belleville area, and might normally be considered part of the Park District's responsibilities, have been entrusted to other hands. There are also several sewage districts created solely for that purpose in the suburban and outlying areas. Fire districts are of the same order, the most important being the Signal Hill Fire District, which serves the part of Signal Hill not incorporated into the city and helps maintain that neighborhood's separate status. Belleville, of course, has a city fire department, as do the municipalities of Swansea, Shiloh, and O'Fallon (all have joint agreements to help each other in case of emergency). True to its Southern origins, Belleville has not rushed to embrace the "special district" concept, instead grafting most of its additional governmental activities onto the existing governments over the years.

There are two other major, organized governmental institutions within the Belleville civil community, both federally supported, which actually represent a fifth set of governments. The first of these is the post office. Strictly speaking, the post office is not a government, but a government agency, although its role in lending coherence to the Belleville civil community by giving Belleville and the area it embraces beyond the city limits a common address makes it of central importance in the delineation of the civil community.

The second is Scott Air Force Base which, although a separate community in many respects by virtue of its military character, has been incorporated *de facto* into the Belleville civil community and has become the catalyst for many of the intergovernmental relationships (both federal-local and interlocal) that have developed in the civil community since the establishment of the base in 1917. With the base a permanent military installation, there has been time and the incentive for the relationship between it and Belleville to grow closer over the years. The substantial impact of the base on the local economy is obvious. The children of base personnel attend the local schools, bringing the service people into at least the formal aspects of community life and aiding the community financially with federal aid to its educational system under the program designed to bring funds to federally-impacted school districts. During the years since 1917, the base and the civilian governments in the civil community have evolved a system of informal government to meet shared problems to the point where the base has simply added itself to the bundle of local governments serving a common population.

In addition to these formal governmental institutions and agencies, the Belleville civil community also possesses a number of public nongovernmental institutions which provide vital and necessary public services to the civil community as a whole and to its constituent parts. Perhaps the most important of them is the Belleville Chamber of Commerce. Created in 1924, it has been functioning for over a generation with varying success as the catalyst for community activities, as chief promoter of economic development, and as the gadfly to stir the formal governments to undertake specific new governmental responsibilities. The Chamber of Commerce is of course primarily the province of the downtown businessmen. Yet among its 800 to 1,000 members are also city fathers, politicians, and even labor union leaders. Indeed, the Chamber's Civic Problems Committee includes representatives of the local labor movement who, together with the business representatives, concern themselves with various civic problems.

The geographic area of service of the Chamber of Commerce, as its leadership defines it, also helps clarify the limits of the civil community, although the Chamber's economic interests go beyond the scope of shared political concerns which give a community its civil, or political, character. The area extends east to include Scott Air Force Base, north to Highway 50, half of the way south to Freeburg and Millstadt (both of which have their own Chambers of Commerce and are substantially independent civil communities), and west to the western limits of Belleville.

In addition to the Belleville Chamber of Commerce, which concerns itself primarily with communitywide economic and political matters, there is the Belleville Community Council which is concerned with communitywide coordination of social, welfare, and cultural activities. The council is almost entirely apolitical and has virtually no contact with the working politicians or political leaders of the civil community. Its function is to coordinate a wide range of local public nongovernmental social improvement programs and welfare organizations, ranging from the various religious welfare agencies to the Philharmonic Society. The council is dominated by people often labeled "do-gooders" by politicians and business leaders. Its lack of visible political significance should not obscure its importance as a public agency providing many amenities for a community which generally attempts to limit the role of formal government in any case. The range of its service activities within its field of specialization makes it no less a quasi-governmental body than the Chamber of Commerce.

Also part of the governmental structure of the Belleville civil community are the less-than-communitywide organizations which include the neighborhood improvement associations and the specialized civic and service organizations. The activities of the latter are much the same as they are in every community. Their memberships are not geographically based, but represent different religious, social, and economic constituencies. They are political or governmental only in the sense that their projects fill gaps in the range of public services provided by government in the civil community, occasionally serve to mobilize support for governmental programs they particularly favor, and by their existence contribute to community loyalties and attachments.

The neighborhood improvement associations developed and were most active in the first period of settlement, after World War II, of the new subdivisions on the outskirts of Belleville, where they were useful devices for helping the new residents overcome the "time of troubles" that generally accompanies the "settling in" of any area. The associations were useful in helping the inhabitants acquire such public amenities as streets and sewers and perhaps in arranging for or preventing their annexation to the city, depending on local sentiments.

After these initial tasks were accomplished, the improvement associations generally drifted into a state of inactivity, having exhausted their major reasons for existence. The problems formerly requiring group effort became individual; the people affected could go directly to their alderman, the mayor, the township supervisors, the council meetings, or other public officials; there was no need to pool their efforts through an improvement association. Nevertheless, several of the associations have remained in existence and have been periodically revived in times of neighborhood-wide need. The South Side Improvement Association is the only one of them that has transformed itself from a troubleshooting organization into what is in effect a social club. It maintains a clubhouse and an artificial lake for its members (those who live in the neighborhood the Association serves) and, as such, retains its strength by filling certain needs which in American society are quasi-governmental.

In several of the neighborhoods that have remained outside the city limits, the volunteer fire departments are the equivalent of the neighborhood improvement associations. They not only provide fire protection but serve as social centers, points of community or neighborhood identification, and as mobilizers of neighborhood residents. When there is an issue at stake most of them also act as lobbying groups.

Even less formal than the neighborhood improvement associations are the unincorporated subdivisions which maintain a certain subdivision identity. Many have little more than nominal cohesion, but even that much seems sufficient to enable the subdivisions to serve as a rallying point around which residents can organize. The prime reason for them to organize is to resist incorporation into the city. These people are members of the civil community in every other respect. Many participate in the various other governmental and quasi-governmental activities of the civil community, from the Chamber of Commerce to the YMCA. They send their children to the community's schools. But they resist incorporation, preferring a style of life which to them is more "rural," and the ostensibly lower taxes that accompany "rural living." Because the topography of Belleville enables its residents to live close to the center of the civil community but away from the city proper in semi-rural "estates," this alternative is a very attractive one. In sum, these people frequently oppose any effort to include them within a municipal jurisdiction because of their commitment to what they conceive to be a rural *style* of life (including the lower taxes) which they desire to maintain even while they are committed to an urban *way* of life.

The governments and public nongovernmental institutions of the civil community are tied together in a rather intricate if very informal network which forms the structural basis of the civil community's constitution and which, as such, provides a variety of governmental and quasi-governmental services implicitly designed to satisfy a wide range of public needs for those who reside in the Belleville area. Not only do those residents, taken in aggregate, have a wide variety of needs, but as individuals their needs are highly varied. Individuals and groups interested in different institutions and seeking to guarantee their maintenance are willing to act on behalf of their particular interests even to the exclusion of others. For this reason they are favorably disposed to maintain a civil community comprising many different governments and service agencies. As it is presently designed, the formal structure of the civil community enables the local residents to utilize only

those instrumentalities that appeal to them or that can be useful
to them, in any combination they desire. Lacking any strong
desire for "rationalization" of government organization, they
value the present civil community arrangement precisely because it allows such a wide range of choice within a common
civil framework. This attitude is clearly indicated in the
evolution of the formal structure in its various parts.

The Evolution of the Formal Structure

The first formal act giving any American city an identity of
its own is its platting as a city. Belleville was platted privately
by the owner of the townsite in 1814, at the same time that it
became the county seat of St. Clair County and while Illinois
was still a territory. Considering the predilections of the predominantly Southern in-migrants who were settling southern
Illinois at the time and who did not favor living in or building
in towns, it is unlikely that Belleville would have come into
existence when it did except for the fact that it was designated
county seat and the county commissioners wanted the courthouse located in a town. Still, the subsequent history of its
evolution as an urban community approximates that of many
other frontier communities that were founded in the greater
West before the coming of the railroads.

As it was, the "town" was a town in name only during its
first five years of existence. Its limited political organization accurately reflected the local situation. Aside from the county
government, which was organized in Belleville in 1814, the
only local official in Belleville's early years was the constable,
first appointed in 1814 by the county commissioners to handle
such local law enforcement tasks as then existed in the Belleville area.

From the beginning the Belleville civil community was
shaped by public nongovernmental institutions, as well as by
governmental ones. The first quasi-public nongovernmental institution in the civil community was organized in 1815. It was

a school established privately by a Yankee missionary who thought it more important to provide a means of bringing literacy to the frontier than to establish a church. The school, supported only by the efforts of the missionary and the tuition payments of the "better class of Southerners" who were concerned with teaching their children to read and write, was the first of a succession of private schools which were the only organized source of education until 1848. Although the schools were privately supported, those who taught in and supported them thought of their work as a public service, and they were considered public servants by the community.

More than one plane of government was involved in shaping the civil community from its begininng. Indeed, the first "organized government" designated to serve Belleville by name was the post office, established by the federal government in 1816. The postmaster, a part-time employee and political appointee, was paid, as was the constable, from fees. The postal station in the corner of the postmaster's private establishment became the center of the town's daytime activities whenever the mail coach arrived.

At about the same time, the county commissioners established a district market on Courthouse Square as the only place where farmers could legally sell produce within the city. This excursion into the realm of local public regulation, characteristic of many Southern communities before the Civil War, was to be maintained by the city government as the city market for two generations. Until the 1890s no independent grocery stores were allowed within the city limits and all retail selling of agricultural products had to be in the city market.

While the county commissioners met at Belleville as early as 1814, it was not until 1817 that the first courthouse was built. In fact, it was the first public building in the city (the post office was still located in a private establishment and the market was little more than a set of stalls). These three public institutions were crucial to the town's development, for at least two of them attracted local residents to the center of the settlement several times a week. Around them a central business district began to develop, with specialized private enterprise supplementing the meager public services available.

In 1819, five years after its establishment and a year after Illinois became a state, Belleville was incorporated as a village, with a municipal government consisting of a village president and council which met periodically to consider such matters as street maintenance and law enforcement. The 1820 United States census indicated that the population of the new village was 150. For the next fifteen years the governmental structure in the civil community remained much the same: a village government whose primary functions were to provide constabulary services and to regulate the village market; the county government (whose functions actually extended beyond Belleville's borders), concerned primarily with minimal road maintenance, law enforcement, and the administration of justice in the name of the State of Illinois; and the federal post office which provided the only major and continuing governmental service to Belleville proper other than the city market, and which served as the major point of contact between Belleville and the outside world.

In 1836 the Germans, who had begun to settle in the area, founded the second public nongovernmental institution of importance in the civil community—the Library Association. Although organized on a subscription basis, the association included a fairly large proportion of the community's residents and provided the requisite library and literary services. It existed as a private library until the early twentieth century, when it was transformed into a public library supported by local taxes to enable Belleville to qualify for a Carnegie Library grant. Belleville claims that, on the basis of the Library Association, it has the oldest library in continuous existence in the state of Illinois.

It was not until the 1840s, however, when the civil community entered its second generation of existence, that there was a concerted expansion of public facilities to serve its people. In

1840 Belleville's population reached 2,000 and the city crossed the threshold into a new era of urban services demanded by a population of increased density. In 1844 a volunteer fire department was organized. The firefighting organization, which received little assistance from the village government, soon expanded into several volunteer companies which, according to the custom of the times, competed with each other in fighting fires. Also in 1844 the county poor home was organized and located in Belleville. The home was the first social welfare institution in the civil community and in the county as a whole.

In 1848 some of the same German settlers who had organized the Library Association twelve years earlier banded together to organize a semi-public school system. The school organization of 1848 consisted of a school board elected by the members of the school association to govern the school system. The schools were financed by land grant funds from the federal government and from private tuition payments. It was not until 1856, in response to changes on the state plane, that a public school system was created.

In 1850 Belleville was incorporated as a city. That same year, after dividing the city into two wards, the citizens elected their first mayor and a four-man council. Belleville received a special charter from the state legislature in 1850 (the standard manner of incorporation until 1872). While it later abandoned that charter to come under the Illinois Cities and Villages Act after 1871, the city has in fact continued under the same form of government since its first incorporation. By 1961 the number of wards had increased to seven, each of which continued to elect two aldermen. The mayor was still elected at large, together with the city clerk and city treasurer. Throughout Belleville's history, no serious effort has ever been made to alter the structure of the city's government.

Additions to the public institutions during the 1850s, together with the changes made in existing ones at the beginning of Belleville's second generation, not only changed the civil community's immediate constitution but had far-reaching effects on its present constitution as well. In many respects Belleville's existence as an urban polity may be said to date from this transition period. Certainly the structure of local government continues to bear the imprint of midnineteenth-century styles.

The newly established city built a combination firehouse-city hall in the early 1850s to serve as its seat of government, occupying it in 1857. The city government remained in the firehouse until its range of services expanded sufficiently to require a larger building to house the city employees. The first separate city hall was erected in 1869 and was used as such until 1959, when the present city hall was completed.

In 1852 some of the new settlers in the area platted their own settlement on the west side of Richland Creek, then Belleville's western boundary. The settlement, which became West Belleville, was incorporated in 1871 and existed as an independent municipality until the two cities were amalgamated by referendum in 1882. The creation of the separate municipality seems to have been more closely related to local topography than to any friction between the residents of the two cities, since they shared the same school district after 1856.

The creation of a school district supported entirely by public funds in 1856 was the last element in the urbanization of Belleville's governmental structure. Coming as it did within ten years of Belleville's incorporation as a city, it completed the foundation of the major governmental institutions which still serve the civil community today. The school district was organized pursuant to the state law of 1855, which provided for the organization of local school districts and for local support of the public schools. In Belleville it relieved the public nongovernmental school association, which had been functioning for nearly a decade, of the obligation to support semi-private schools for the citizens of the entire civil community. The present Belleville district functions under the laws that succeeded the Law of 1855.

The post-Civil War years were ones of great expansion of local government services and activities throughout the United

States, with changes coming primarily in the direction of professionalization of personnel and the introduction of more "sophisticated" urban public works. Belleville was no exception. In the late 1860s a small beginning was made toward the creation of a full-time cadre of public servants in the city. In 1867 a police department was created, with permanent salaried police officers. In 1878 the fire department became semi-professional when the hiring of a salaried chief and one or two salaried deputies to train and guide the volunteers was authorized. The volunteers continued to be the mainstay of the department's operations. The skeletal framework for other departments also developed in the period after the Civil War. In the meantime, in 1876, the city reincorporated under the new Illinois Cities and Villages Act to take advantage of the act's ostensibly more liberal benefits.

The 1890s brought some new developments and the abandonment of an old function. In 1890 the city market became less important when the establishment of independent grocery stores was authorized by city ordinance. The spread of retail grocery services and the decline of direct selling by farmers soon ended the life of the city market, and it disappeared before the turn of the century. During the same period St. Clair County adopted township organization (a midcentury Yankee import in northern Illinois which took root very slowly in the Southern-settled areas of the state), thus adding another formal government to the emerging structure of the Belleville civil community. First St. Clair Township and then Belleville Township took over responsibility for general relief, township roads, and local law enforcement from the county government, which heightened the separation between the Belleville civil community and St. Clair County as a whole. In fact, it is likely that St. Clair County adopted the township system in order to further the separation of its already culturally very divergent civil communities, allowing the townships to serve as political buffers between the different local communities and the county as a whole as well as enabling those local communities to better control functions previously centralized in the hands of the county commissioners.

With the opening of the twentieth century, the expansion of both local government and government locally in the Belleville civil community became a regular and continuing phenomenon. At first governmental expansion reflected a restructuring of the existing government institutions on an expanded basis rather than the creation of new ones. The expansion took place in all parts of the local governmental system. The city and township governments began to concern themselves with highway improvements. The existing private toll road companies began to abandon the field to the public authorities who, at the same time, were beginning to feel the pressure from local automobile owners for better roads. Between 1902 and 1917 the remaining toll roads passed into city, township, or county hands, and their improvement as public highways was begun. In 1911 the first permanent post office building was dedicated. In 1916 a public library was built with the aid of Carnegie funds, and the library became a public-supported institution.

By World War I Belleville had also begun to expand its governmental system structurally. In 1916 the Belleville Township High School District was created, adding a public high school to the local school structure. The high school was created on a township basis, but by its charter was allowed to include more than two townships. From the beginning it was the local government that came closest to delineating the actual area of the civil community, far more so than the city alone. Indeed, its boundaries were soon to become virtually coterminous with those of the civil community. In 1922 Belleville's park district was established, the last of the structural additions of the period.

It was not until 1946 that another major governmental activity was added to the civil community's range of services. That year the Belleville Township Junior College was organized. Since then, all further expansion of government has taken place within the existing framework, either through the creation of new agencies such as the Planning Commission (1961) or through expansion of the functions of older agencies.

Since the founding of Belleville, the general trend has been to expand governmental services and activities in such a way as to provide a wider range of public services and to provide them with increasing sophistication, expertise, and professionalization. Since the founding of the city this expansion has been promoted somewhat reluctantly by the local influentials (or at least a majority of them), but it has taken place nonetheless.

There is a generational pattern in the history of this expansion.[2] The first decade of Belleville's existence as a civil community saw the initiation of such fundamental governmental activities as rudimentary law enforcement, the administration of justice through the court system, the regulation of certain aspects of local commerce, the establishment of postal service, the creation of a self-governing municipality, and even rudimentary education facilities, all through the creation of appropriate, if limited, governmental or public nongovernmental structures to handle them. A generation later these rudimentary facilities were expanded in a second wave of governmental structural development, revolving around the establishment of a city government and a permanent public school system. After yet another generation, rudimentary professionalization of government services was initiated and a body of full-time local government employees began to appear on the scene. A generation later the new twentieth century brought a great expansion in the range and intensity of local public services provided by government. In subsequent chapters we will see that the second generation of the twentieth century has, in the period since 1949, continued this pattern of generational increments in governmental expansion by other means, in response to the demands for governmental activity which had accumulated in the intervening years.

Belleville's Constitution: The Other Ingredients

The character of Belleville's politics is partially shaped by its formal structure as a political entity. It is shaped further by the unique combination of motivations in the Belleville civil community. Given certain prior influences of its formal constitution, a civil community's politics are generally motivated by four basic factors. First is the ethos of the community, the goals and standards against which the community measures itself—what might be called the community's "ethical constitution." To a great extent this ethical constitution determines which issues are raised in the community and how they are defined. Second are the cleavages that make the community what it is and the social base on which these cleavages rest—the "sociological" or "economic" constitution. It is the sociological constitution that determines how issues are handled by its determination of the distribution of power in the community and the interests to be protected. Third is the community's "foreign policy"—the relationship it envisions for itself and that it desires to maintain with the surrounding communities and with the world at large. Fourth is the community's policy and attitude toward conservation and change, the dominant attitude of its citizenry toward problems of growth and citizens' reaction as a community to the pressures internal and external changes force upon it.[3]

Even the limited amount of information available makes possible some generalizations about Belleville's political motivations. With respect to Belleville's ethical constitution, the civil community is not untypical of many medium-size American cities. Bellevillians appear economically conservative, strongly partial to the middle-class way of life as it is generally practiced in the United States, proud of their rate of home ownership and the high level of skills to be found among the local population, strongly pro-"education," and generally proud of Belleville as "a good place to live and raise one's children." Belleville is a civil community that boasts of its cultural attainments, ranging from its library to the Philharmonic Society (which has been in existence since the 1830s and which claims to be the oldest in the United States), from its schools to its bookstore (the only full-fledged bookstore in St. Clair County).

To the outside observer it appears to be an orderly community. One community leader says: "We have a lot of Germans here, and Germans respect authority and are easy to govern." The police records appear to reenforce his view by indicating that 75 percent of the city's juvenile delinquency comes either from juveniles who do not live in Belleville or from those whose families have moved in from East St. Louis in recent years. Belleville's public aims are relatively simple. Its articulate citizens desire to maintain this way of life with as little change as possible while still keeping pace with a changing world.

Belleville's sociological constitution is built around the two major cleavages in the community described in Chapter 2. The Catholic-Protestant cleavage remains the major one in local political life. An aspect of old Belleville, it is moderate in its impact and is reckoned with politically thorough ticket-balancing in all spheres of electoral activity, the equal distribution of political rewards in most other spheres, and the consideration of the interests of the two subcommunities as such in most aspects of public activity. The geographic cleavage between the East End and the West End is fast becoming a second major sociological cleavage as the West End becomes the preserve of immigrants from East St. Louis while the East End remains the preserve of old Belleville. This cleavage is likely to intensify in the future. Today it is manifested in differing community loyalties which, with a few exceptions, have yet to be translated into political loyalties. Thus many of the new settlers in the West End still consider themselves to be "citizens" of East St. Louis, where many of them work or own businesses. At the present time, the East St. Louis newspaper has the largest newspaper circulation in the West End, while Belleville's own *News Democrat* is naturally predominant in the East End. A small number of political leaders active in the East St. Louis-based Democratic organization have been elected to precinct posts in the West End, where they do not fit into the traditional Belleville pattern of political behavior. Their influence is partly counterbalanced by the many civic and business leaders of East St. Louis who have moved to Belleville's West End to get away from the atmosphere of the former city and who favor the traditional political behavior patterns of Belleville.

A third cleavage may be said to exist in Belleville, although it remains politically latent and is not likely to become pronounced in the near future. Underneath the spread of politically articulate and represented Bellevillians there exists a substratum of politically inarticulate groups, almost none of which has sought to be politically articulate at any time in the recent past.

Ever since its origin, Belleville has built its foreign policy around a central principle—isolation from the American Bottoms. Since the late nineteenth century this has meant, in reality, isolation from East St. Louis and East St. Louis's interlocking pattern of politics, vice, and crime. Bellevillians particularly fear three things from East St. Louis. First of all, they fear an invasion by East St. Louis Negroes. There is a generally unobtrusive but powerful anti-Negro bias in Belleville, which is related to the city's proximity to the high concentration of Negroes in the American Bottoms and which leads to an undercurrent of fear that the Negroes may some day "break into" Belleville and settle there.

Second, there is the tremendous fear of the East St. Louis style of politics, a style typical of the classic urban "machine" and one which tolerates a great deal of open graft and corruption and even more "honest graft" and political cronyism rarely associated with "good government." Belleville's leaders are very careful to keep East St. Louis politics and the politicos who represent it from entering their city's limits. Some leaders in Belleville are fearful of the settlement of East St. Louis people in the West End, believing that it will pose political problems and a threat to the old Bellevillians' control of the city once the new people get settled and seek to participate in local politics.

Third, and perhaps most immediately important, is Belleville's fear of infiltration by the "syndicate." Organized crime, whose control of vice, gambling, prostitution, and the like in the American Bottoms is popularly acknowledged, has been kept out of Belleville throughout most of the syndicate's existence, with the single exception of the period in the 1940s prior to the Calhoun reform movement (see Chapter 4). The encroachment of the syndicate in the city during those years frightened the leadership of Belleville and most of the residents of the city, apparently to the extent that constant vigilance is now maintained to keep any hint of syndicate operations outside of the city's boundaries. The Belleville police force, which was reformed to eliminate alleged syndicate influence, maintains a twenty-four-hour vigil in this respect. The mayor has issued standing orders for the commonly recognized leader of the syndicate to be arrested if he should so much as drive across the Belleville city line, even if he can be held for only a few hours. It is felt that this will discourage him from coming into the city. The same is true in regard to his leading henchmen. The Belleville police department keeps an up-to-date record of the automobile licenses issued to all known syndicate figures in the St. Louis metropolitan region, and its patrols keep their eyes open for the presence of any of the automobiles registered in their names that might drive across the city line; they too are stopped on sight.

In the years since 1945 Belleville has been propelled onto the metropolitan frontier. It is unlikely that Belleville would have chosen to be so propelled had the choice been offered it. However its location on the fringe of the St. Louis metropolitan region left it no choice. Belleville is ideally located for suburbanization, being on the first line of expansion out from East St. Louis. It lies at a convenient commuting distance from St. Louis. Belleville's reputation as a nice community is an added attraction. Those people from the Bottoms who had made a little money and wished to live a more comfortable and prestigious life on the bluffs began to move up to Belleville. Scott Air Force Base is another force propelling Belleville; it not only provides an economic boost to the community but also brings in new residents, permanent and transient. As a result of these forces at work, Belleville has undergone considerable numerical growth since the end of World War II (see Table 8), a growth which has had to be managed, whether the community originally wanted it or not.

TABLE 8

Settlement, Incorporation, and Growth of the City of Belleville

Date of first plat	1814		
Date of incorporation	1819		
Date of arrival of railroad	1871		
First paved road connection	1921		
	Population		
1850	2,941	1910	21,122
1860	2,520	1920	24,823
1870	8,146	1930	28,425
1880	10,683	1940	28,405
1890	15,361	1950	32,721
1900	17,484	1960	37,264

Belleville's leaders realize that without some growth the community would wither. They simply wish to turn the growth to Belleville's advantage as a community, that is, to enhance its local self-sufficiency. They have therefore been making an effort to attract new industries to the area to provide the employment and economic base necessary to assimilate the growth that has taken place, to provide local employment for as many of the local residents as possible, now and in the foreseeable future.

Local Politics and Patterns of Partisan Allegiance

Belleville's response to the four factors mentioned earlier is reflected in its political history as a civil community. When the Germans arrived in Belleville in the 1830s they found an essentially virgin political field in a community just beginning to assume an urban identity. Thus, unlike many other immigrant groups who had to serve out their generation-long period of Americanization first, the Germans entered local and state politics almost immediately. At that time, with Jacksonian Democracy at its height, the majority party in the state and nation was the Democratic Party, which certainly was the majority party in southern Illinois. The Germans became Democrats and advanced rapidly, both within the Belleville civil community and as St. Clair County's representatives to Springfield and even Washington. The first mayor of Belleville after its incorporation as a city in 1850 was of German background. Of the thirty-nine mayors who have served the city between 1850 and 1962, a majority have been of German descent.

The Germans in Belleville, like their brethren in most other parts of the North, became Republicans at the time of the Civil War, responding positively to the challenges of abolitionism and national survival. The idealistic aspects of the Republican ascendancy were especially relevant to many of the Germans who settled in Belleville, particularly to those who were products of the "Latin peasant" movement, an urban back-to-the-land movement which originated among German intellectuals in the Old Country and which had motivated many of the first Germans to settle in the Belleville area. These "Latin peasants" were neither Latins nor peasants, but were educated men who brought with them the liberal ideas that characterized a major portion of the intelligentsia of early nineteenth-century Germany. Many of their ideas found fertile ground in the United States and led to a general German sympathy with the North and the antislavery movement in the dark years of the Civil War.

The Republican commitment was strong in both Belleville and in St. Clair County as a whole from after the Civil War until the turn of the century. Then the industrialization of the American Bottoms brought in Southerners and European immigrant groups who entered the ranks of the Democratic Party. Belleville, however, remained solidly Republican. It is said by political old-timers that the only Democrat in the Belleville area elected to public office between 1900 and 1930 was the minority representative to the state legislature (whose position is virtually guaranteed by the state's cumulative voting system). While World War I tended to reenforce the Germans' Republicanism nationally, as a rejection of the Democrats' "responsibility" for leading the war against Germany, Belleville was not particularly affected by this sentiment. Germans in Belleville were at least neutral during World War I, if not actively opposed to the country of their forefathers. It was during World War I that German ceased to be taught in the public schools, and it has been only since World War II that the language has been reintroduced. The Germans and the rest of the Bellevillians remained predominantly Republican until 1928.

As it did in so many other parts of the country, the combination of Prohibition and depression shook, then broke, three generations of party loyalty in Belleville. The initial enactment of the Prohibition amendment and its enforcing legislation did little to weaken the German attachment to the Republican party because Prohibition was initiated as a bipartisan issue. The Germans, who enjoyed their beer and were very disappointed to see their breweries and beer gardens closed down (in point of fact, one of the two local breweries remained open throughout Prohibition), were most disappointed with the new state of affairs but at first could only blame both parties equally.

As the 1920s wore on and the Democratic Party became the party of "repeal," that party became more attractive to the traditionally Republican Bellevillians. The break came in 1928 during the Al Smith campaign. Smith, who was both a "wet" and a Catholic, was a very appealing candidate to some voters for both reasons. Belleville voted Democratic in the presidential election for perhaps the first time since the eve of the Civil War. The coming of the great Depression in 1929 forced the issue, and in 1930 a Democrat was elected to Congress locally with the support of most Bellevillians.

The coming of the New Deal in 1933 reenforced this trend toward the Democratic Party by winning labor over to the Democrats. In this connection the WPA, providing money and jobs, was important locally during the heart of the Depression. As the 1960s began, the Democratic Party was the strongest and best-organized party in the civil community. There was a consistent Democratic superiority over the Republicans, by margins of approximately seven to four, in most, if not all, partisan elections.

Central to Belleville's structure of electoral management is a system of not quite ad hoc local parties. City and township elections are contested through these local parties. Belleville's local parties are only partially continuing bodies. Their names are changed every two years to avoid the necessity of holding primary elections under Illinois law. While there is some continuity in their leadership from one election to another, the general pattern of local politics makes serious continuity for more than two elections unusual.

The parties are organized through a "ticket" system. Mayoralty candidates are informally nominated or approved by the leaders of the local representative oligarchy (see Chapter 4). They then become the heads of tickets with the right and obligation to select candidates to run under their party's designation for the other offices to be filled. The heads of tickets also determine the party name, and by and large they have the first and final say as to who will be on the ticket with them. These tickets are balanced so as to reflect the basic political divisions within the civil community, that is, between Protestants and Catholics and between representatives of the business community and representatives of the labor unions.

The most characteristic feature of the Belleville local party system is the widely accepted tradition of individual movement from party to party, which is maintained by active political participants. Parties are reorganized through realignments, "dropouts," and "switches" from one election to another. Realignments take place when different interest groups make common cause with each other and change their alignments from one election to the next. Dropouts occur when elements previously active for one group simply abstain from participating in city or township elections to avoid committing themselves or offending anyone. Finally, some of the politicians, particularly the professional politicians and precinct committeemen, simply switch from one side to another, not out of principle, not for the sake of a different alignment, but because they get a better deal, either in money or in patronage, from one side than from the other.

The latter course of action is directly related to the tradition of paying precinct committeemen for getting out the vote. This is not considered to be "buying" the election, since under the ground rules in Belleville, a precinct committeeman is a "professional" political organizer who has a "right" to be paid for the time he spends in working his precinct and to be able to pay his workers as well. Therefore the precinct committeeman negotiates his support on the basis of what he will get paid, unless he is required by the county organization to which he is related to support one ticket or another.

Before each city election two or perhaps three tickets are developed. Campaigning is done by ticket; the candidates for election to city and township offices are listed on the ballot under their respective party labels. Between elections these parties cease to function, since their "affiliates" have no real commitment to them or to each other. Internal politics between elections in Belleville is ward politics in which aldermen from the various wards compete with one another for benefits, or cooperate with each other for their mutual benefit.

What of the two national parties (or more accurately, the

two state-county parties which use national labels)? Their role is quite limited in local elections. They know that open interference on their part usually works against the ticket they wish to support. At the same time, they do have a stake in Belleville elections because the city elections are also township elections and the various factions in the regular county parties need the Belleville township supervisors and assistant supervisors in their struggle for control of the county board. Regular party labels have never been used in Belleville elections insofar as is known locally, but the regular parties will discreetly support one ticket against another if they find it to their advantage to do so. Even so, they mix in only when township supervisors are being elected.

St. Clair County politics is dominated by strong political organizations based in the heavily populated, working-class, industrialized American Bottoms. The leading organization is that of East St. Louis "Boss" Alvin Fields. In the late 1950s and early 1960s it was challenged by the organization of Elmer Touchette, based in Centerville Township. As old-style political "machines," neither organization appealed to many Bellevillians. Nevertheless, the fight between the Fields and Touchette groups was carried over into Belleville, as well as into the rest of St. Clair County, although to a lesser degree, where it was confined to the struggle for control of the township offices. In 1961 three aldermen in Belleville were also precinct committeemen, due to their allegiance to the Fields group. Touchette's faction controlled several precincts in the West End, in an area adjacent to Centerville Township, the faction's base of operations. In the 1962 election the Fields supporters carried Belleville handily. Most Bellevillians consider them to be the lesser of two evils.

There is little incentive for the regular party organizations to mix into Belleville local politics. The jobs available in the city hall may be good for prestige, but they are not particularly valuable as sources of income or power. Outside of the police and fire departments there is no merit system in City Hall, but the strong union ties of the civilian employees almost guarantee them tenure. The mayor appoints department heads, the city attorney, and his own secretary, and no more. Others are appointed by the aldermen when vacancies occur. Changes in the administration do not mean wholesale changes in jobs in the city government. Consequently most of the positions available to a victorious candidate for patronage are voluntary positions on civic boards and commissions which carry some prestige and more responsibility, but furnish few, if any, opportunities for monetary gain. And power is, after all, concentrated in the local oligarchy, not in the city hall.

Although the city hall is across the street from the county courthouse, relations between the two are seriously strained and are kept to a bare minimum. One finds virtually no contact between the city and the county, and learns very little about the government of either from the officials of the other.

The desire of Bellevillians to maintain the separation between city politics and the politics of the rest of St. Clair County acts as a powerful bulwark against regular party intervention. This separationist impulse extends even to the point of insisting on separation where the same people are involved in both city and county politics. Thus the precinct committeemen who were active either for the Fields or Touchette groups did not appear to carry that activity over into their aldermanic positions. On the contrary, they themselves have compartmentalized their activities quite clearly and were encouraged to do so. It is very likely that, had they not, an intensive campaign financed and led by the local civic leadership would have been waged to unseat them.

The separation between city and county-state politics tends to be something of a one-way street. Several mayors of Belleville have moved up to the state legislature after leading the city. The state senator in office in the early 1960s moved up through the ranks after starting as police magistrate in Belleville. However, Jerome J. Munie, the previous mayor, was the only county official to have been subsequently elected to city office. Munie was the exception because he is reputed to have been one of the two honest sheriffs in the history of St. Clair County. Whether this is true or not is obviously difficult (or impossible) to determine, but such was his reputation locally. He was supported because he represented honesty at the county level, where honesty is considered most difficult to maintain. Yet even he was elected only because the local oligarchy was split three ways in the campaign.

It is essential to remember that city politics in Belleville is for all intents and purposes "clean." This is certainly true in comparison with politics in the remainder of St. Clair County. This is not to say that there is no "honest graft" in the city hall. Opportunities abound for making money on the side, for doing things which are legal only in the strict sense of the term, and a man who is willing may get several offers every day he is in office. At the same time, if a man rejects such offers in no uncertain terms and is labeled "incorruptible," the potential sources cease to present themselves or bother him. Such "incorruptibles" are not punished politically, either. On the contrary, their public support generally grows when their choice becomes known. On the other hand, serious "corruption," when it is discovered in time, usually has meant defeat in the next election.

NOTES

1. Eugene J. Webb, Donald T. Campbell, Richard D. Schwartz, and Lee Sechrest, *Unobtrusive Measures* (Chicago: Rand-McNally, 1966).

2. See the discussion of the generational pattern in American politics in Daniel J. Elazar, *Toward a Generational Theory of American Politics* (Philadelphia: Center for the Study of Federalism, 1970).

3. This approach follows the seminal work of Norton Long, as expressed in his "Aristotle and the Study of Local Government," *Social Research* 24:3 (Autumn 1957); and his "The Local Community as an Ecology of Games," in *American Journal of Sociology* 64:3 (November 1958).

PUBLIC
INSTITUTIONS
AND THE
STRUCTURE OF POWER

The Oligarchy and Its Span of Control

Three basic forms of political control can be identified in contemporary American communities: *autocratic, oligarchic, and polyarchic.* Under the autocratic form a single individual or an organization functioning as a corporate person (for example, a local industry in a company town) exercises virtually complete control of the community by being decisively involved in every significant community decision. Today this type of control is rare in the United States, surviving in a few small communities in the South, the mountain West, the Appalachian Northeast, and the American Bottoms.

Oligarchy is a form of political control in which a substantially closed group of individuals, or interests represented by individuals, enjoys a virtual monopoly of power by retaining within its confines decisive control over significant community decisions. Oligarchy, in its various forms, is undoubtedly more prevalent in American communities than is the autocratic form. The simplest form of oligarchy involves rule by a *single element,* a small group with the same fundamental interests, whose members are closely linked together through a network of

Sources for this chapter are listed in Appendix B.

interlocking relationships. To those outside this type of oligarchy, its rule seems no different from that of an autocracy. Inside the controlling element, however, decision-making is collegial, if only because no individual is in a position to exercise control on his own. The other two forms are more complex. One combines the leaders of a number of different elements in the community in the decision-making group, but the group itself remains self-selected and still stands in more or less autocratic relationship to the remainder of the community. Since each element in the coalition has its own sources of power, none is able to decisively influence community decision-making without the others. At the same time, the more elements represented in the oligarchy the more open it becomes to various points of view in the community. A *multiple-element oligarchy* can be broadly based, quite responsive at least to the articulate publics in the community, and representative of the great majority (if not all) of its significant elements. In that case, it can be considered a *representative oligarchy,* or one which, in exercising decisive influence over community decision-making, gives every legitimate interest a share, albeit a highly structured one, in the process.

Polyarchic systems of political control are those in which no single individual, group, or element, nor any exclusive combination of them is able to monopolize power or to be decisively involved in every important community decision. Polyarchy is characterized by relative openness and fluidity to the extent that power is not only widely diffused but different issues or situations are likely to change the influence of different groups, thus giving them greater or lesser roles in the decision-making process, depending on their salience. Moreover, leadership within these groups is more likely to change with some frequency. Organized *polyarchy* may be said to exist where elements, groups, and individuals active in the community are mobilized in routinized ways and exercise their influence through recognized channels. Since their participation is expected, coordination among them is possible on a regular basis. Where power is even more widely diffused and the participants less easily coordinated, a *fragmented polyarchy* exists. In a fragmented polyarchy it is difficult for both participants and observers alike to determine who has the power to achieve their goals. If sufficiently fragmented, a polyarchy may become chaotic, but since *chaotic polyarchy* would signify a community in dissolution, it is a rare phenomenon.

Belleville is governed by a representative oligarchy. The civil community has apparently been governed by an oligarchy of this kind since its emergence as an entity. The various elements in the oligarchy usually function in partnership with one another, although periodically there are conflicts within the structure. Belleville's representative oligarchy is so well established locally and so easily definable that the civil community may well be considered a paradigm of that form of political control on the local plane.

Belleville's representative oligarchy is made up of three component elements: business, labor, and the politicians, each of which is internally balanced along religious lines. Within itself, each element is broadly representative of a major segment in the community. Together they provide representation for the interests of the great majority of Belleville's people on most issues. The persistence of their power attests to this as well as to the neat alignment of economic and religious cross-pressures characteristic of Belleville's oligarchic structure.

Evidence of the oligarchy's near monopoly of the power exercised by local forces within the civil community is striking. It is visible in case after case of local political decision-making. One of the most clearcut examples of that power is the fate of the recent sewer construction program. It represents a "hard case" in that the oligarchy exerted its power even though it was not clearly speaking for a majority of the local public in its actions.

Like most communities with growing peripheries, Belleville

Autocracy	Oligarchy	Polyarchy
Politician-dominated	Single element oligarchy	Organized polyarchy
Industry-dominated	Industrial-business-political oligarchy	Fragmented polyarchy
Business-dominated	Representative oligarchy	Chaotic polyarchy

Exemplary Design:	Exemplary Design:	Exemplary Design:

FIG. 2.   Forms of local political control

desperately needed new sewage lines and treatment facilities. As the members of the oligarchy and others tell the story—with considerable relish—they recognized this need. In a series of informal meetings, representative businessmen, trade union leaders, and politicians drew up a sewer plan. The united oligarchy then presented its plan to the city council for formal adoption. Under legal provisions requiring a referendum only upon petition of 5 percent of the voters at the last regular election, the council arranged to float the bond issue needed to finance the project without going to the people.

At that point a local dissident group, the Belleville Homeowners' Association, which opposed the sewer program much as it has continually opposed any program that might lead to a rise in property taxes, started to circulate petitions to bring the matter to the public for a vote. Realizing the referendum could possibly go against them, the oligarchy immediately mobilized to stop the petitions before they obtained enough signatures. They started a rumor to the effect that the signers of the petitions would have their names printed in the newspaper, thereby exposing them to unpleasant publicity. The local newspaper itself deliberately encouraged this rumor by denying it in print. That was all that was needed. The opposition group was never able to obtain enough signatures on the petition to bring the matter to a referendum, so the sewer program was implemented.

Whether or not the oligarchy spoke for a majority of the citizenry in this case cannot be known. The truth of the matter is that the potential division on this issue was not between the community leadership and "the people," but between the "cosmopolitans" (in the classic sociological sense) in the community who perceived the necessity for a sewer construction program as vital to the community as a whole, and certain "locals" who, in the absence of immediate benefits, could not see the importance of the program, particularly vis-à-vis an increase in their property taxes. It was in order to avoid the possible consequences of this division that the oligarchy acted as it did, in this case with considerable success. Its success was due substantially to the fact that its stand remained broadly representative of the interests it represented. No single socio-economic segment of the community united to oppose it (the opposition faction drew some strength from all segments on the basis of localistic attitudes), and the oligarchy is organized so as to represent social and economic groups, not cosmopolitans and locals as such. Its leadership is drawn overwhelmingly from among the cosmopolitans in each socio-economic element, as is the case with most "permanent" leadership groups. If it had not been broadly representative in at least this sense, it is quite likely that the oligarchy would have lost its fight.

The oligarchy does not function simply to support the downtown business interests who happened to take the lead in developing the sewer program. It supports the interests of all its components and, consequently, the interests of the bulk of the politically articulate elements in the community. For example, in 1961 Belleville completed a new city hall. The building's heating plant uses coal rather than gas or oil because the labor elements in the local oligarchy demanded that coal furnaces be installed to provide additional work for the local coal mines and miners. The business and political leaders in the oligarchy acquiesced to this even though most of them felt as individuals that a more modern form of heating fuel should have been used.

The scope of the oligarchy's power is not limited to any particular government or public nongovernmental institution. Its representatives screen all candidates for major offices in all the governments of the civil community, particularly for the city and township offices of Belleville proper and for the various local school boards, and they often recruit candidates as well. Screening and recruitment of candidates are two different matters. Both are important parts of the electoral process that assures the maintenance of the local political system. The recruitment of candidates may be either active or passive. One element in the tripartite oligarchy may actively seek men to run for specific offices, or men may come forward to run by seeking the support of one of the elements prior to a screening by the others. In any case, the proposed candidates, regardless of the origins of their candidacy, are screened three times—by the downtown business group, usually functioning through a screening committee of the Chamber of Commerce; by the labor unions, functioning through the Union Label Committee; and by the city hall politicians.

When a candidate passes these screenings and is approved by all three elements, he has no difficulty getting elected to office. Consider the last three mayors. In 1949 H.B. Calhoun was elected by a big majority after having been asked to run by the business leadership and approved by labor and more than half of the political leaders. He served two terms, and in 1957 Jerome J. Munie was elected to replace him. In this election there was a division within the oligarchy (a not uncommon development in certain electoral matters where competition is tacitly allowed unless it is felt that it would endanger the system). In this case, the division was stimulated by the desire of

one exceedingly influential downtown businessman to run for
the office. The business community backed him. Labor, joined
by most of the politicians, backed Mr. Munie, and the cosmo-
politan reformers from all three elements who had coalesced
around Mayor Calhoun during his term of office backed a third
candidate. Munie, with the backing of two-thirds of the elements that usually make up the oligarchy, won by a narrow
margin.

Because Mayor Munie was ill during the last year and a half
of his term, Charles Nichols, then an alderman, became acting
mayor. When election time came, Nichols was asked to run
for mayor by the newspaper, acting on behalf of the business
leaders. Mr. Nichols agreed and was quickly endorsed by the
other elements. As a union man he had no difficulty obtaining
the endorsement of labor, and as a veteran alderman who was
well acquainted with the city hall politicians he got their endorsement handily. He won the election by 8,000 votes to his
opponent's 3,500.

Despite the power it obviously possesses when it functions
in a united manner, the oligarchy is neither monolithic nor all-
powerful. It will divide on specific issues when the interests of
various elements conflict and then re-form without apparent
difficulty. When this happens proposals from any one of the
elements can be (and often are) beaten by the voters at large.
Indeed, even when the oligarchy is united, if its leadership
misreads the will of the majority, it is likely to be beaten in
referenda. This ever-present possibility acts as a check on the
leaders who form the active oligarchy and helps keep them
more or less responsible to the larger public. The articulate
elements in the community will also indicate their disapproval
of projects before the referendum stage is reached. Three
recent issues illustrate this.

In 1959 two local businessmen began to agitate for the construction of a municipal airport. They were not supported by
the bulk of the business oligarchy, but were sufficiently influential themselves to secure a pro forma Chamber of Commerce

endorsement of the idea. At that point the business oligarchy rallied behind them, if only for appearances' sake, and the Chamber of Commerce actually agreed to pay for the referendum required to establish an airport authority and to issue the bonds for construction of the airport. The Chamber of Commerce did pay for the referendum, but the proposal was defeated. Here the oligarchy itself was divided. Labor was opposed to the airport as an unnecessary drain on the taxpayers for the benefit of a few businessmen. The politicians did not care and the business community itself supported the project only half-heartedly. Here, then, the oligarchy itself reflected popular majority opinion and the decision went accordingly.

Shortly after the airport issue, the oligarchy reunited to promote urban renewal. An urban renewal committee was created, broadly representative of business, labor, and the politicians, and began to make plans for renovating one of the older neighborhoods in the city. The committee knew that urban renewal was a new and frightening concept in a community that still refused to adopt a zoning ordinance for fear of restricting "property rights," so they made every effort to do their planning secretly before mounting a public campaign for its acceptance. But word leaked out and, led by the Homeowners' Association, there was a popular outcry of disapproval, less because of taxes than in opposition to urban renewal as a program, as the public understood (or misunderstood) it. The members of the oligarchy, realizing that they would be defeated on the issue which of necessity had to be placed before the people for a vote of approval, backed down. In 1962 they tentatively and very cautiously renewed their efforts.

Also in 1962, the oligarchy lost a referendum. A large school bond issue, designed to improve and enlarge the facilities of the township high school and junior college, was proposed. It was widely endorsed by all the recognized leaders in the community—the Chamber of Commerce, the labor unions, and the PTAs (which are very powerful in school affairs). The proposition had the full and active support of the local newspaper,

the city hall politicians, and, of course, the school board and
school officials. It was given ample publicity. Nevertheless, it
lost, apparently because it ran up against the perennial reluctance to raise taxes. The willingness of the people of Belleville
to seek other leaders or to take matters into their own hands
when they disagree with their regular leaders, helps keep the
oligarchy representative, although obviously the "power of the
people" is confined generally to vetoing the oligarchy's proposals, and is rarely the power to initiate programs directly.

The Character and Composition of the Oligarchy

A closer look at the components of Belleville's representative
oligarchy—its fundamental economic interests, spokesmen, organizations, religious affiliations, and political ties—is in order.
The lines of political power drawn in the following pages represent an effort to summarize the local power system. The very
effort implies a degree of order in what is in reality a much
less structured, more chaotic, and certainly less consciously
organized system. Though not as neat as portrayed on the
printed page, the lines of power in Belleville are quite tidy,
indeed, unusually so, relative to those of other communities.
Perhaps this is a reflection of a penchant for organization which
was brought into the community by its German settlers.

The business element is perhaps most visible in civic leadership roles, since it is made up of people who are concentrated
in downtown Belleville and who are publicly recognized as
civic leaders. The prime movers in the business community are
generally drawn from the ranks of five institutions or professions: the bankers, particularly from the First National Bank of
Belleville; the building contractors; the realtors, who are ex-
ceptionally powerful locally, because they are able to pre-
empt places which their counterparts in other communities
must share with major local industrialists who play a lesser
role in Belleville; the local office of the Chicago Title and Trust

Company; and the Belleville *News Democrat.* These five are regularly represented because they expect to be. Changes in leadership personnel reflect changes within the five. The spokesmen for the bankers, for example, may be drawn now from one bank and now from another, depending on the individuals available for service.

Clearly the groups from which Belleville's prime movers are recruited reflect the "main street" character of the town's economy. The major business concerns in the community revolve around retail trade and the buying and selling of land and real property. Perhaps because of its small scale and diversity, industry, though extensive, is not regularly represented per se; the various industrialists who are active in the community are active as individuals rather than as representatives of their particular industries. In their case it is much more clearly a matter of individual choice as to whether or not they participate in civic affairs.

The business element, including the active industrialists, functions in large part through the Chamber of Commerce which comes closest to being its institutional "home." The Chamber, however, is not exclusively representative of the views of "business." The Chamber's leaders, particularly the professional managers, conceive of their organization as having a major role to play in the development of new public services and in the improvement of established ones. Its professional managers in particular accept their organization's quasi-governmental role and often seek to reflect a broader public. This means that the Chamber functions as both a pioneer and a gadfly vis-à-vis the considerably more conservative response of the local governments, whose elected officials are extremely cautious when it comes to changing the status quo. Not infrequently the Chamber's interest in expanding public services is not in agreement with that of the oligarchy or even of its business segment. The airport issue is a case in point. In such cases, its leaders must work hard, if discreetly, to convince the element which ostensibly supports them. Whether or not they succeed, they are generally given reasonable opportunity to make the attempt.

The overall position of the Chamber of Commerce in the community has undergone some change since the opening of the metropolitan frontier. For several years prior to 1949, there was a sharp, if temporary, cleavage between business and labor. Insofar as the Chamber of Commerce spoke for business, the City Council, which generally spoke for labor, would be at odds with it. This considerably reduced the Chamber's influence in the community at large. Even during that period, however, individual businessmen from among the leadership group were careful to disassociate themselves from the Chamber and did function in harmony with the unions in dealing with specific issues.

During that period, and partly because of its "unharmonious" stands, the Chamber fell on bad days. It was reorganized by the business leaders as part of the general revolution in Belleville after 1949 and under its new professional management it has consciously sought to work in harmony with labor and the politicians. Significantly, the Chamber does not always back the United States Chamber of Commerce on issues in which labor has taken an opposing stand, because it does not wish to antagonize the local unions. It has opposed the U.S. Chamber's stand on right-to-work legislation, for example. As a result of this conscious effort to develop a harmonious relationship, labor is now more kindly disposed toward the Chamber and participates with it in numerous civic activities. Labor even has representatives on some of the Chamber committees (those with a clearly "communitywide" focus), and the Chamber has gone out of its way to include them on committees which deal with civic problems or economic development.

In 1961 the Chicago Title and Trust Company was relatively new on the Belleville scene. It was then perhaps the one major outside business interest that played a direct role in civic affairs.

A few years earlier it had bought out the local title and trust company as part of its statewide plan of expansion, which led to its indictment by the federal government under the anti-trust laws. Chicago Title and Trust does not like to be openly involved in community affairs, but it has its man in on everything that might concern it.

The Belleville *News Democrat* is the end product of a series of newspaper mergers dating back to 1858. Although the newspaper is properly considered to be part of the business element in the oligarchy, in some respects it maintains an independent position and can be considered as an element in and of itself. Owned by a local family which has been in the newspaper business for many years and which is noted for an aggressive outlook, the newspaper is politically powerful locally. Its politics are independent Democratic and it supported President Eisenhower in 1956. In general, its stands are progressive and liberal, civil libertarian, humanitarian, favorable toward social welfare programs, and always in favor of what are normally considered forward-looking actions in the local community. The *News Democrat* is particularly positive in its orientation toward education, never failing to emphasize the educational institutions in the community and to give them exceptional coverage. The newspaper was one of the major elements that helped trigger the reform era of Mayor Calhoun. It was strongly pro-Calhoun and more recently pro-Nichols and has continued to support Nichols vigorously.

In the early 1960s the leading realtors and bankers were Protestants. It is unclear whether this is traditional or not. The large downtown retail merchants tended to be Jews. This has been the pattern for many years. Nonetheless, individual Catholics are to be found in all three categories.

Generally, the business element, like the rest of Belleville, tries to stay out of county politics. When it must get involved, however, then it tries to choose the faction that seems the lesser of evils. In the early 1960s Belleville's businessmen tended to support the Fields organization, partly because it was the faction in power and partly because Touchette had a particularly unsavory reputation.

Organized labor is the second element in the representative oligarchy. Unionization is so extensive in Belleville that the policemen, firemen, and "civilian" city employees have been unionized for a generation. Belleville remains the only representative oligarchy among the cities of the prairie in which organized labor is visibly and openly an equal partner and does not have to rely on being represented through some other group. The Belleville Central Trades and Labor Council embraces all the local unions and serves as the central agency for union labor in the civil community. The Union Label Committee is responsible for screening candidates for labor endorsement, a task it fulfills with great dedication.

Unlike the business community, which prefers to exert influence by securing appointive positions on boards and commissions and whose members are willing to run for elective office in the realm of school government only, the laboring people are willing and active candidates for city and township elective posts. The township officials include several active unionists, as does the city council. Of course, organized labor is represented on every relevant board and commission as well, and the various unions involved virtually control the inspection boards that deal with their respective crafts. The teachers have been unionized since 1940. Mayors Calhoun and Nichols were both educators. Nichols was one of the organizers of the local teachers' union.

Politically there is no single strongest union in Belleville, just as there is no single strongest industry. Probably the teachers' union and the city hall employees' union are the most influential in politics. The teachers are active because in a political culture which never taught them that teachers should not be actively involved in politics, that is, that politics and education should not be mixed, their middle-class orientation stimulates their feelings that they "ought" to be involved, and their jobs give them both the time and (in Belleville) the organization necessary. The city hall employees are active because they have a direct economic stake in government, as well as a sense of political concern by virtue of their jobs. The coal miners were influential at one time, but the decline of the industry has lessened their influence accordingly.

The third element in the oligarchy is the collection of city and township politicians known as the "city hall crowd" or simply as the "politicians." They are organized around the city clerk and the city treasurer, the two "permanent, full-time" elected city officials (in the sense that they are regularly reelected to office as long as they choose to run) who have a stake in city hall beyond that of the mayor or the councilmen, if only because they tend to hold office indefinitely and to rely on their offices as their primary sources of income. These two officials and their immediate supporters are the only politicians substantially uninfluenced by pressure from other elements in the oligarchy. Clustered around the city hall politicians are the precinct committeemen and others active in city politics, most of whom have primary commitments to other interests. The city hall group also includes the city hall employees, who have dual loyalties to their union and to their quasi-political positions in the city hall.

The politicians maintain an independent position of power in the oligarchy by virtue of their being at the fulcrum of formal and informal power in the civil community. They are the ones who choose to devote time to securing such a position — and, in this way, are duly rewarded for doing so. Otherwise, they are rarely men of individual stature in the community at large, except for the one or two at the top, the mayor and the local member of the state legislature.

Essentially there are three groups of politicians active in city politics. There is the city hall group centered on the "permanent" officeholders mentioned above. There are the precinct committeemen attached, in the main, to one county organization or another, who align themselves with the ticket in local elections for pay or for other political reasons. Third, there are the handful of civic leaders recruited from the business community. While they do not run for public office at the city and township level, they help determine who the candidates will be and who will be elected and who are willing to serve on the boards and commissions. They stand out from their colleagues by virtue of their specifically political, as well as general civic, interest in local affairs. They are willing to become involved in what is referred to, often contemptuously, as "politics"; consequently they have a substantial voice in decision-making in the city government.

It should be noted that the perpetual and periodic opponents of the oligarchy also have an organization around which to coalesce. The "antis" are found mostly in the Homeowners' Association, originally formed during rent control days as an anti-rent control lobby. At that time most of the city's real estate dealers were connected with it. Since rent control passed from the scene, the organization has been declining. Its revenue comes primarily from the home show which it sponsors every year. Furthermore, its membership has been changing as those identified with opposition to local change and to possible tax increases have become more powerful within the organization. The change has been abetted by a common "vicious circle": as the organization became more "anti," it lost more of its older members; as it lost these members it had to attract newcomers from among the natural "aginners"; as the "aginners" increased in power the organization became increasingly isolated from leadership of the community, and its "anti-ness" was reenforced.

Although the Homeowners' Association's interests are based primarily on the self-interest of the small landlord who wants to keep his property taxes down, it also takes certain quasi-ideological stands on behalf of limited government. For both reasons it serves as a rallying point for the opposition to the oligarchy, particularly for the locals in the community who do not view issues in terms of their effects on the community as a whole, but instead are concerned with the immediate effect on their pocketbooks and their neighborhoods.

The Structure and Functions of the City Government

Belleville has a weak-mayor system of city government. The mayor's job had not been considered a full-time position until Mayor Nichols decided to devote full time to the office because he felt city business required it. Since the mayor received an annual salary of $7,000 in the early 1960s—a sum sufficient for him to live on as far as he was concerned—and the incumbent did not seek to become wealthy, it was possible for him to spend all his time on the job. Nichols' decision to do so was, in effect, an extension of the reform movement and represents a second stage of the revolution in the political life of Belleville, in which reform of the status quo and the initiation of new programs are becoming secondary to the effort to raise the caliber of the governmental organization designed to implement the new programs (see Chapter 5).

Taking the long view, the office of mayor has become more powerful over the years. Until 1867 mayors were elected for one-year terms only and although one or two served more than one term (but not consecutively), tenure in the mayor's office was, as a rule, brief. Between 1867 and 1931, mayors were elected for two-year terms. The first mayor to serve more than four consecutive years was Fred J. Kern, who served from 1903 to 1913. Since then it has happened several times. Four-year terms were instituted in 1931, making this more feasible.

In Belleville mayors traditionally have reflected the city's outlook. Whether by design or not, the last four incumbents have been alternately Catholic or Protestant. Mayor Nichols is a Protestant; his predecessor was a Catholic; Mayor Calhoun was a Protestant, and his predecessor Catholic. The two most recent mayors have been identified with organized labor and the previous two were unquestionably sympathetic to labor.

At the same time, the last three mayors have been acceptable to (if not endorsed by) the business community. However, none of them were either blue-collar workers or businessmen. In recent years mayors have been chosen from professional or semi-professional occupations. Calhoun and Nichols were educators, and Munie was a professional public servant and politician.

The mayor is empowered to prepare the city budget, but in reality he has little control over the budget that is adopted. Mayor Nichols has exercised as much control as he can by requiring that department heads submit budget requests to him before they are submitted to the city council. Nichols reviews them and attempts to trim the budget as he sees fit but when the budget goes to the council, the department heads can go to the council's finance committee and have the cuts restored. What the mayor has tried to do is set absolute limits on expenditures and allow the alderman to divide up the pie within those limits as they wish. Even this tactic has had only limited success.

The city is heavily in debt, some high officials say hopelessly so. Indeed, one of the consequences of the reform movement has been to increase the city's debt substantially. The new services and the upgraded activities cost money and since Mayor Calhoun's day more money has been spent by the city than has been taken in. The problem is aggravated by two conditions, neither of which is subject to the mayor's control and one of which is not even subject to the city's control. First, the system of aldermanic courtesy leads to the adoption of all pet projects proposed by the individual aldermen for the wards, constituents, or interests they represent. The mayor can do nothing to prevent or limit this. Aldermanic courtesy has not been touched by reform. It appears as if the city council, whose members are primarily concerned with their own projects, has acquiesced to the reform movement as long as its basic prerogatives are not disturbed.

All things considered, the mayor functions as the city's

chief executive primarily by force of his personality and by his ability to operate politically. The mayors who have been able to exercise personal leadership and who have been successful in handling the council and the citizenry have been able to achieve much during their terms in office. The others have been mere figureheads.

The remainder of the city's executive branch is divided into nine departments, four of which (police, fire, health, and recreation) are responsible to separate quasi-independent boards. The street and sewer departments, the sewage plant, cemetery administration, and city engineering department are the only ones directly responsible to the city council (through its committee system) and the mayor. Thus of the nine departments in the city government, only five are directly controlled by the elected representatives of the city.

The very structure of city government in Belleville, as it has evolved, tends to increase agency specialization even within the municipal government itself. The city council is responsible primarily for maintenance programs and for overseeing the housekeeping affairs of the city. Except in its ordinance-passing (actually ratifying) function, it has relatively few concerns that touch on new activities and new programs, or that require considerations for long-range planning. By and large, it merely keeps continuing programs up to date.

The city council operates through the classic "congressional" committee system, under which power is rarely exercised by the council as a whole. The standing committees check their counterpart departments and make decisions which are then, in effect, ratified by the council. The major interests of the city council are streets, sewers, and streetlights, despite its theoretical power to deal with a wide range of governmental concerns. This de facto abdication of power by the central policy-making institution of the civil community's only major multipurpose government tends to reduce the city government to the level of a special district. This specialization is primarily a result of the focus of constituent pressures on the city council and the weight the aldermen assign to those pressures. The city's residents contact their aldermen for street repairs, sewer extensions, better street lighting, but for little else. Since the aldermen rely on the casework they do for their constituents as the means by which they become known, popular, and reelected, they focus their attention on the areas with the most direct public relations payoff. These highly particularistic concerns of the city council as a body are reenforced by the essentially "localistic" frame of reference of the aldermen, primarily working class locals whose interests are relatively constricted to begin with.

There are fourteen standing committees on the city council. Two—the Buildings, Grounds and Parks Committee and the Cemetery Committee—concern themselves only with maintenance. The former oversees the maintenance of the city hall and other city structures, as well as the two city parks and the latter has the responsibility for maintaining the cemetery and expanding its grounds when necessary.

Four other committees are basically overseers of the city administration. They are the Claims Committee, the Finance and Audit Committee, the Judiciary and Legislative Committee, and the Public Relations and Personnel Committee. The Claims Committee handles city payments, Finance and Audit passes on the budget and oversees the expenditure of city funds, Judiciary and Legislative handles the drafting of city ordinances and the supervision of the city's relationships with the courts, and Public Relations and Personnel handles public relations and makes appointments to jobs. These are also basically housekeeping bodies.

Three committees have regulatory functions: the Utilities Committee which supervises such local regulation of the utilities as exists; the Ordinance and License Committee which supervises the issuing of licenses that fall under the city's purview; and the Health and Sanitation Committee which reviews the rather limited work of the city health department.

Finally, five committees are at least nominally concerned with continuing programs. The Civil Defense Committee is ostensibly responsible for overseeing the civil defense program which, since it is nonexistent, places that committee in virtually inactive status. The Sewage Disposal and Sewer Lines Committee has some involvement in the present sewer construction program although the program is, by and large, handled by one of the citizens' commissions. In general it oversees the maintenance of the sewage treatment plant and the existing sewage system. The Traffic and Parking Meters Committee handles matters which come before the city council from the traffic department. It is perhaps the only one that must concern itself with advance planning to a significant degree. The Police and Fire Committee ostensibly is responsible for police and fire matters, but since there is a Board of Police and Fire Commissioners that actually controls the police and fire departments, and a Police Pension Board which handles their pension matters, this committee is also left with little to do. The Streets and Bridges Committee is probably the most active single committee in the city government, other than the Finance and Audit Committtee; street programs, which are of major concern to the aldermen, are channeled through it.

By and large, then, the city council is limited to handling the maintenance and housekeeping chores of the city government. By its own choice it takes little aggressive action and plays a minor role as policy initiator. Its members display little desire to enter other fields; they apparently are content to handle the tasks set before them, leaving the more glamorous programs and the problems of policy initiation to the citizens' committees and the permanent boards and commissions.

The permanent boards and commissions manned by volunteers appointed by the mayor have become equally, if not more, important than the city council in the management of the city's affairs, and clearly more important in making policy for the city government and the civil community. In Belleville, as in many other civil communities, they have become, in effect, a third branch of the city government, if not specialized "second houses" of the local legislature. Their power is further enhanced because they more directly reflect the local oligarchy and are indeed directly representative of it. Moreover, the programs they are concerned with require considerably more expertise than those handled by the city council. The boards and commissions may be divided into two groups—the regulatory boards with quasi-legislative and quasi-judicial functions and the quasi-independent administrative boards. Among the regulatory boards are the Building Code Board of Appeals, the Gas and Plumbing Code Board of Appeals, the Utilities Board of Appeals, the Board of Electric Commissioners, and the Police Pension Board. The first four handle the regulation of construction in the city and the utilities serving the city. The last supervises the administration of the police pension fund. The first four boards, while probably representative of the community leadership, tend to be dominated by the groups they regulate in a manner quite common in American government at all levels.

There are four semi-independent administrative boards in the Belleville municipal structure whose members are appointed by the mayor. By custom each board includes labor, business, and professional representatives. The Board of Health is responsible for the management of existing local public health programs. Belleville's Board of Health does not maintain programs of the scope found in most of the larger cities in Illinois. Essentially it confines itself to providing the sanitarian services required by state and federal law. The Board of Police and Fire Commissioners supervises the administration of the police and fire departments. Its membership is typical of that of most of the city's boards and commissions, and includes a dentist, the president of a local stencil company, and the president of one of the local unions. This group is one of the most independent in the city's structure. The Library Board manages the Belleville Public Library with virtually a free hand.

Because it has its own tax levy, the Playground and Recreation Board is legally the most independent board. Its members are generally able to manage their recreation program as they see fit. They appoint the employees of the recreation department and the director without interference. By custom, the board includes representatives from the local school boards. It is one of the few city agencies that embraces parts of the civil community beyond the limits of the city proper. Perhaps because of its larger concerns, the Playground and Recreation Board has shown considerable initiative in recent years by expanding into the area of park management. The director of the recreation program is primarily responsible for the creation of Citizens' Park, a voluntarily created and supported fifty-five-acre park outside the city limits.

Since these quasi-independent administrative boards function with considerable independence, they are also in a position to hire most of the higher civil servants with professional training who work for the civil community. The Board of Health's sanitarian, the police and fire chiefs responsible to the Board of Police and Fire Commissioners, the librarians who serve the Library Board, the recreation director responsible to the Playground Board represent the hard core of professional expertise available to the city government of Belleville. However, because they are responsible to independent boards and commissions, their weight is not directly felt in city hall.

In addition to the city council and the permanent boards and commissions, there are six citizens' committees which serve Belleville. Advance policy formation insofar as there is any in Belleville and the responsibility for the development of new programs rest in the hands of these citizen's committees, which are appointed by the mayor from among the local leadership. They take upon themselves the tasks of formulating plans, programs, and projects prior to their formal consideration by the city's elected officials, who are often placed in the position of merely ratifying the committees' decisions.

The first of these is the Advisory Committee on Master Sewer Plan Financing. It handles the planning and public relations for the city's major project of the 1960s, the extension of the sewer system, and has been responsible for planning and directing the implementation of the sewer plan. The Citizen's Committee on Urban Renewal Redevelopment also deals with a major program, though because of the adverse publicity that attended its first efforts, it has just begun to develop an action program.

The Citizen's Committee on Flood Control is responsible for developing a project to control the flooding of the lower sections of Belleville by Richland Creek, another program of great local interest. The flooding, which appears to have worsened as population in the area has grown and which has disrupted normal drainage patterns, must be dealt with in some way, either by evacuating the residents—an obviously unpopular method—or by getting money from the Army Corps of Engineers and the Soil Conservation Service to put in a flood-control project. In 1962 the committee was working on the latter possibility.

The City Plan and Zoning Commission was created to formulate a city plan and prepare a city zoning ordinance for adoption. Belleville has had no professional planning assistance and, as of 1962, had no zoning ordinance, although the matter of zoning had been considered and debated for twelve years or more. (The committee was in the final stages of preparing a zoning ordinance for submission to the city council for adoption in 1962, and one has since been adopted.) In addition it has worked with the other advisory committees to prepare specific program plans which are being put together as the city master plan.

The Civil Defense Committee is the preserve of a handful of community actives with a particular interest in civil defense and is charged with the development of what is ostensibly to be a major local program. Civil defense in Belleville, as elsewhere in the United States, has not attracted local support; accordingly the committee's functions are limited.

The Legislative Committee is not responsible for the administration or development of any single major project, but has a continuing task of some importance. It is concerned with problems of intergovernmental coordination, primarily with the state but also with the federal government. Its major concern is the maximum utilization of the services of Belleville's state senator and the area's Congressional representative in Washington to gain benefits for the civil community. Since most of the major projects presently being planned and implemented in the civil community involve state and federal aid, the committee's scope of action is constantly being enlarged.

It is clear that a governmental system as diffuse as that of Belleville reenforces the power of the informal leadership, in this case, the representative oligarchy. All governments are reduced to the status of special purpose governments and all except the city council are actually controlled jointly by representatives of business, labor, and the city hall politicians, in various proportions. It is paradoxical, but the appointed boards tend to be much more representative than the elected council. The city council is also less potent because it tends to be highly specialized in its membership and not very representative of the community's different interests. The council finds itself in this position in great part because of its own choosing, a "choosing" which has gone on bit by bit over the past hundred years, but which is implicitly ratified by each new council. The aldermen make little effort to get involved in the activities of the boards, commissions, and citizens' committees unless the activities of the other agencies interfere with council prerogatives or prejudices.

There is a common complaint among the politically aware "progressives" in the community that Belleville has no high-level, trained professionals in the city hall, other than the police and fire chiefs. This is literally true; that is, in the city hall proper those two officials are the only ones professionally trained and permanently committed to their lines of endeavor. At the same time, there are other professionals in the city who are dispersed among rather widely separated departments—

including the sanitarian, head librarian, recreation director, to name the three most prominent ones who are at least formally connected to the city's government. Outside of the formal structure of the city government there are still others. The school administrators, for example, are a highly professionalized, powerful group in the community. Even so, the progressives are more than half right in their assessment. There are no government-employed professionals concerned with the civil community, or even the city, as a whole—no city manager, administrative assistant to the mayor, city planner—in short, no urban generalist who must look at the overall picture. The only professional concerned with the civil community as a whole in the early 1960s was the manager of the Chamber of Commerce. In line with the recent trend among Chamber of Commerce professionals, he viewed his role as that of a professional gadfly for the civil community, if only within the general sphere of interest of Chamber of Commerce members, namely the promotion of efficiency, economy, and economic development. He construed the Chamber's interests broadly, serving as a pacesetter for his lay leadership as much as their servant. However, he felt lonely in lacking any counterpart to talk with in city hall. Without similar generalists strategically located at other points of influence in the governmental structure of the civil community, one man's voice is of limited effectiveness.

Politics in the Other Governments

Politics in Belleville Township is tied so intimately to Belleville city politics that it does not need to be considered separately and at length. Township supervisor and assistant supervisor candidates run on tickets set up by the mayoralty candidates and are held accountable along with those tickets. Although they apparently use regular party designations when serving on the county board, they are elected within the local party system, and for all intents and purposes are locally nonpartisan. This is possible because party allegiance, formally speaking, is not important, even on the county board. The two rival organizations in St. Clair County are both Democratic, but they are the only ones with any power and are supported by ostensible Republicans as well. This gives them not only the image of nonpartisanship, but control of the minority Republican Party as well.

The functions of Belleville Township are virtually extensions of the city's municipal functions. Since it is a city township, it has no responsibility for roads. The township administers the general assistance program, which means that it is of great concern to the labor element in the community. Traditionally some of the township supervisors are union men. By the same token, the business community has very little interest in the township government and is quite willing to leave it in the hands of labor and the politicians. The division of power and positions within the township government is between these two elements of the oligarchy, with the tacit acquiescence of the third element so long as township officials confine themselves to the routines of township government.

The township also manages city and township elections. This role gives it the authority and power to redistrict the city's precincts, which it did in 1961 at the same time the mayor and city council redistricted the city's wards. Since both of these are primarily concerns of the city, the functional integration of the township officials into the city's government is nearly complete. The township offices are located in the city hall to further enhance this integration.

Each of the other townships in the Belleville civil community has developed a quasi-independent political subsystem of its own. Most undertake to provide a few more services for their residents, chief among them the maintenance of township roads. This function varies in importance, depending on the extent of urbanization of the townships and the existence of local municipalities within their boundaries to handle most of the local streets. However, it does remain a function of some importance to people who settle in the new subdivisions.

In most of these townships politics is half local and half county in orientation, with the county organizations concerned with township politics only to the extent that they wish to control the county board and need the votes of the township supervisors. Otherwise, like those in Belleville, the citizens of most of the townships, particularly those to the south and east, want to be free of the influence of East St. Louis. While they are generally less successful than Belleville because they can mobilize less countervailing power, they do attempt to keep township politics as local as possible. Their limited success is evident in the houses of prostitution and gambling establishments within their boundaries, "protected" (or undisturbed) by the sheriff's patrol and effectively outside the township's jurisdiction.

St. Clair Township, whose outer boundaries remain those set down by the original federal land survey of southwestern Illinois, is something of an exception in that it has quasi-municipal powers. The township, which virtually surrounds (and once included) Belleville, and embraces the Village of Swansea, encompasses the greater part of the civil community outside of the city limits. Over the years it has acquired certain regulatory functions which give it effective control over local building and plumbing codes that influence the character of urbanization within its limits. It possesses municipal powers for the passage of ordinances, as well as control of the regular township functions.

The central executive and enforcement agency of St. Clair Township is the town board of auditors, which meets monthly. The board drafts the township's ordinances and enforces its regulations ostensibly at the behest of the town meeting which, under Illinois law, retains formal legislative authority. Despite its exceptional position it would be erroneous to overestimate the importance of St. Clair Township, whose limitations are best understood when it is realized that its 1962 budget was approximately $81,500.

While school politics is perforce formally divided among

the six elementary school districts and the high school and junior college district which serve the Belleville civil community, in fact there are many points of similarity among all the districts in the functioning of their political subsystems by virtue of their common inclusion in the same civil community. By and large, politics on the elementary-school level is based on the activities of the parent-teacher associations and the teachers' union. The PTA in each school district openly endorses and campaigns for candidates. Legally the teachers' union must refrain from active participation in school politics, but it does campaign quietly for individual candidates whom it interviews and endorses. The union's right to do so is tacitly accepted by the community.

The teachers' union is quite strong. It was organized in 1940 by a group of educators who felt that the teachers did not have sufficient job security and were not being adequately paid. The union struggled in its early years, but, in a union town, was ultimately successful. It has been instrumental in securing passage of tenure laws in all the local school systems and the establishment of merit systems, better wages, and fair promotion policies. It has been supported by local organized labor and opposed by the Illinois Education Association, which is more attuned to the interests of the school administrators.

School elections are easily managed by the PTA and the Teachers' Union because invariably they are low-turnout elections. This is true despite the heavy newspaper publicity given each election by the education-conscious *News Democrat*. While the PTAs and the union endorse and campaign for candidates, they do not select them. Candidates decide to run on a personal basis, file independently, then secure formal endorsements. In some cases prospective candidates use an informal pre-clearance system in which they informally contact the important leaders in the PTA or the union prior to filing.

The religious issue is not overtly important in school politics, but it is clear that a balance is struck by tacit consent. District 116, which includes most of Belleville and part of Swansea, elected two school board members in 1962. Three ran for the vacancies—a Presbyterian, a member of the German wing of the United Church of Christ, and a Catholic. The first two were elected. In District 119, the Belle Valley district (a considerably smaller one), the two board members up for election were both unopposed incumbents. One was a Catholic and the other a Presbyterian. This appears to be the common pattern.

Religion is sufficiently important in the selection of school board members that the newspaper articles giving the candidates' backgrounds and qualifications include their church affiliation. The only exception is in the Signal Hill District, District 118, where religious affiliations are not mentioned because the important criteria there are status and socio-economic position. What is emphasized in the campaigning for Signal Hill school elections are the candidates' occupations and the colleges from which they were graduated.

Over the past several years members of the liberal professions have been clearly favored by the voters. In general it is the upper middle class that furnishes the bulk of the candidates for school board positions in all districts. Within the upper-middle-class category, white collar and professional people tend to predominate, followed closely by businessmen.

The politics of the high school and junior college district is more complex. It is based on a number of factions, each of which demands representation on the school board and is more or less guaranteed that representation. Among the factions is the pro-athletic group which supports the high school and junior college athletic program. The Teachers' Union is another faction, although here too it cannot be involved officially. The union supports candidates its leaders have interviewed and approved. Those candidates automatically get the endorsement of organized labor. There is no PTA at the high school and junior college level, so the PTA, as such, is automatically excluded from active political participation.

In addition to factional demands on the school board, there are also sectional demands. Belleville proper is guaranteed representation by general consent. The Fairview Station area always has its representatives. By law two board members must come from the unincorporated areas. The entire arrangement conforms to the pattern of government by representative oligarchy found in the civil community as a whole. As in the case of the grade-school districts, the candidates are generally drawn from the ranks of business and the liberal professions, although the factional and sectional distributions tend to lessen the upper-middle-class composition of the board to some extent by forcing the inclusion of representatives from other segments of the community.

While the political subsystems of the Belleville schools are not directly tied in with city and township politics, they are tied to the general structure of community power. Within them, groups not active in city politics have their say because they indicate an interest in having a say. This, in itself, reflects the representative character of Belleville's oligarchical structure of community power. In the case of school politics, those concerned with the schools are as involved in political wheeling and dealing as any other local political actives, but because their interest is specialized, they are given a specialized voice.

Intergovernmental Relations

In truth, intergovernmental relations should not be treated as a separate category on the Belleville political scene, since the whole process of government in the civil community is permeated with intergovernmental relationships and contacts, and mutual responsibilities between government on all planes. There is, however, some value in looking at the relationships among the various governments in the civil community and the other governments around it and above it as separate phenomena.

Interlocal cooperative programs within the civil community are limited to those areas in which cooperative services have been clearly demonstrated to be of mutual advantage. These services are of two types. On the immediately local plane the civil community has a network of interrelated fire-protection agreements which even extend outside its limits. Belleville, Swansea, O'Fallon, Shiloh, Lebanon, and Scott Air Force Base have agreements to come to each other's aid in cases of fire or similar emergency. Within the civil community, Belleville has for several years provided part of the sewage system needs of Swansea. Swansea, an independent village with its own street department, fire department and police force, does not welcome structural integration with Belleville, but makes use of Belleville's facilities, in this case out of necessity.

Since the Calhoun administration, Belleville has had a policy of not extending any of its services beyond its city limits. The city uses municipal services as an inducement to attract new subdivisions to agree to annexation. This policy has been called into question by Mayor Nichols, who does not seek further annexation to the Belleville municipality on the grounds that it costs more to annex new areas than the new areas bring in through taxation. He would like to see the extension of services by contract, but has had difficulty persuading the local leadership of the virtue of changing their policy. The business community, in particular, with its idea of rationality and efficiency, accepts annexation as a basic principle of sound urban organization and opposes anything that might weaken Belleville's ability to enlarge its boundaries. Since the oligarchy is divided, the issue is a standoff and the status quo is maintained.

A step taken early in the 1960s opened entirely new possibilities of interlocal collaboration in the St. Louis metropolitan region, including the Belleville area. The Bi-State Transit Authority, created by the states of Illinois and Missouri at the behest of leading citizens in St. Louis and on the Illinois shore to examine and take action on problems of public transportation within the metropolitan region, won the right to purchase and operate the public transportation systems on both sides of the river. This effort at metropolitan areawide government affects Belleville directly since Belleville is tied into the regional public transportation system by several bus companies which go from downtown Belleville to downtown St. Louis, including one company whose president is one of the leading influentials in the Belleville civil community. In 1962 the bistate agency was just beginning to operate the transit system.

In addition to formal arrangements for interlocal cooperation there are numerous less formal cooperative relationships. They range from ongoing though not formalized cooperation among the local police departments throughout the metropolitan region (perhaps the most continuous and intensive cooperation of all) to the ad hoc cooperation stemming from the needs of a particular moment, such as that involving Belleville's access to the Air Force and the sonic boom question. There is a predisposition among local officials in Belleville to cooperate with anyone except the officials of East St. Louis and St. Clair County, when the necessity for cooperation is perceived. However, their cooperative activities are not perceived as such in any systematic way.

Belleville's relationships with Illinois are close and continuing. On one hand there are repeated local efforts to gain assistance from the state, though it is generally agreed that Belleville as a community does not demand much from the state government. The state senator from St. Clair County, a Belleville resident who is very active in local politics, handles the requests made by Bellevillians.

Most of Belleville's public requests to the state are either for better highway facilities or for state assistance for local construction projects. Two examples will bear this out. In the 1950s Belleville was left out of the interstate highway system as planned by the Bureau of Public Roads and the American Association of State Highway Officials and ratified by Congress. The Belleville oligarchy, realizing the necessity for every city that hoped to make progress in the economic realm in the future to have a four-lane, divided, limited-access connection with the interstate system, immediately contacted state highway officials to begin negotiations to acquire such a connection to the interstate highways of East St. Louis and St. Louis. The product of their efforts was Illinois Highway 460, which not only serves admirably in lieu of a direct location on the interstate network but which was built even before the region's share of the interstate system.

Belleville's subsequent efforts to gain federal assistance for its flood control project led it to turn to the state as well. The federal government required that Belleville pay 10 percent of the project cost. Belleville, unable to raise the necessary amount locally because of its poor financial situation, asked the state to provide the matching funds. Through their state senator the leaders of the Belleville community arranged a series of meetings with the Illinois Budgetary Commission and its chairman to review the project and their request for legislative consideration.

Perhaps the most significant relationships between Illinois and the Belleville civil community are those that move from the state downward. The hand of the state is felt in almost every aspect of life in the civil community. The state regulates the utilities and transportation facilities which serve Belleville and sets standards for local public health services, for the public schools, and for numerous other local government activities. In a typical year (1962) local officials of the Belleville civil community were engaged in fighting a requested water rate increase before the state regulatory agency; were involved in the proper transfer of the local bus lines to the jurisdiction and control of the Bi-State Transit Authority, a state-created and supervised body; were trying to meet the demands of state health authorities for a proper sewage-disposal system to serve the new subdivisions; and were responding to state pressures for further school district consolidation—to mention only the headline questions.

Even more important than the regulatory and supervisory functions of the state officials are the activities of Southern Illinois University in the Illinois segment of the metropolitan region and, to a limited degree, in Belleville itself. In the late 1950s Southern Illinois University undertook to provide the impetus needed to encourage the citizens of Madison and St. Clair Counties to deal with the problems of metropolitanism and social change that had descended upon them. While most of the university's work has been concentrated in East St. Louis, where its first branch campus was located and where its community development division was first established, or later in Edwardsville, where its permanent campus was built, the university has also made itself available to Belleville by offering advice and technical assistance for specific problems. In 1962 the head of the university's community development office in East St. Louis lived in the Belleville civil community. He personally made himself available to the Belleville leadership to work on their planning, zoning, and urban renewal problems, as well as to give general advice, counsel, and assistance on other matters. While SIU's activities have been concentrated on the effort to renovate and revive East St. Louis and have consequently not been directed toward Belleville, in this respect they have also served as a catalyst for the more stable and better developed community on the bluff.

In addition to the foregoing, the state provides continuing financial support for many local programs. Table 9 shows the range of local programs so assisted.

While the federal government does not play the same role as the state in overseeing, supervising, or regulating most of the activities that go on within the civil community, it is nearly as ubiquitous and considerably more visible. This is partly because federally aided projects, by their very nature, are better publicized since they tend to be more spectacular than ordinary local government activities. Moreover, in the case of Belleville this visibility is heightened by the presence of Scott Air

TABLE 9

State Payment Programs Assisting Belleville, 1957-1962

Education

common school fund
transportation
education of handicapped
special tuitions
county supervisory services
junior colleges
normal schools
school lunch and milk*
vocational education*

Highways

motor fuel sales tax
federal highway aid*

Public Welfare

categorical assistance*
Public Welfare Administration*
general relief
care for children

Health and Hospitals

local health services*
tuberculosis hospitalization
hospital construction*
hospital and medical services*

General Local Government Support

sales tax rebate**

Miscellaneous and Combined Services

county veterinarians*
airport construction*

---

* Includes federal funds.
** Enacted since 1957.

Basic sources: *State Payments to Local Governments;* U.S. Census Bureau, *Census of Governments,* 1957 and 1962.

Force Base. Federal activities in the Belleville civil community must be divided into two segments—those carried on by the federal government locally (simply by the existence of Belleville as part of the American political system), and those special activities that revolve around Scott AFB.

The history of federal involvement in Belleville dates back to the establishment of the post office in 1816 as the second governmental institution in the then frontier village. This was followed by the federal land survey of southwestern Illinois, which was the foundation for all subsequent land use in the civil community. While several federal or federally aided activities developed slowly during the nineteenth century, the first major federal impact locally that is remembered as such by the local residents was the establishment of Scott Air Force Base in 1917. Scott was one of the early flying fields of the Army Air Corps in the days when flying fields were established on the Illinois prairie rather than in the southwest. It became a major installation within a short time and began to have a significant effect on Belleville's economy. Some time after World War I efforts were made to close the base, but Bellevillians rallied and, making use of their influence in Congress, they were able to get the Army to keep the base active. After World War II it became the headquarters for the Military Air Transport Service (the device that saved it for Belleville for a second time), and has since become a major Belleville "industry." As such it has really become a component element in the Belleville civil community.

During World War II and immediately thereafter relations between Belleville and the base deteriorated. There was a lack of cooperation between them; servicemen stationed at the base became fair game for prostitutes and gamblers. As part of the civil community's general reform movement and at the instigation of the business leadership operating through the Chamber of Commerce, a joint committee made up of leaders of the local community and ranking officers at the base was formed to deal with mutual problems. This institutionalized face-to-face contact between the civilian and military leaders made it possible for the two groups to discuss their problems calmly, without the earlier back-and-forth recriminations, and to take action, usually successful, to meet the problems. The result has been the virtual elimination of serious civilian-military friction between Belleville and the base.

The Scott-Belleville Committee, as the joint committee is called, is believed locally to have been the first of the town-military committees now common throughout the country wherever there are military installations. Whether this is true or not, the local committee was one of the first of its kind. The good relations it has fostered between the base and the civilian community have had important consequences locally and even beyond. As it stands now, most of the local government agencies in the civil community are represented directly or indirectly on the Scott-Belleville Committee, whose civilian component is dominated by representatives of the oligarchy. The base, in turn, is represented by its top-ranking officers.

One consequence of the restoration of good relations between the base and the townspeople was a redoubling of Belleville's efforts in support of the facility. Local leaders regularly lobby for the base through Congressman Melvin Price. This, of course, meets with the hearty approval of the people in the Air Force committed to the base's operations.

The relationship between the base and the town is so good that in 1962 when the St. Louis metropolitan region was suffering from the effects of sonic booms coming from Strategic Air Command bombers flying high over the area, people in other communities who knew of the relationship contacted Belleville for assistance. Bellevillians took the matter up with the base, which in turn contacted Washington and made arrangements to work out a successful compromise between the needs of the Air Force and the desires of the local residents.

The next major increment of federally aided projects in the civil community came during the Depression. The activities of the federal government during those years are well remembered by political actives in Belleville, many of whom, as union men, benefitted directly from these selfsame federal projects. Workers hired through the WPA created what was then Belleville's major park. They replastered the old city hall, enabling it to last another quarter century. WPA workers built the high-school stadium, swimming pool, and tennis courts, which are available to the whole community. As a labor town Belleville generally accepted this federal aid as useful and necessary.

World War II ended the activities of the WPA, and it was not until the postwar period that the civilian federal government was again felt as a visible presence in the civil community. Even before the advent of the "Great Society," Belleville received federal aid for its sewer projects and flood-control program. In addition, Bellevillians became active in the Kaskaskia Valley Association which was lobbying for federal assistance to create a nine-foot channel on the Kaskaskia River which would reach as far as New Athens, nine miles south of Belleville and which would give Belleville a river port bypassing East St. Louis. (Whenever Belleville can bypass East St. Louis it will work to do so.)

Aside from these attention-getting projects, such less visible agencies as the Federal Housing Administration have been very important in providing the mortgage guarantees and financing for the housing that has been built on Belleville's suburban frontier. These quiet, continuing activities sometimes lead to important changes in local patterns in their own right. One of the most important aspects of recent state-federal cooperation in a matter affecting local community development concerns the FHA. In an effort to curb the spread of improperly planned subdivisions, state and federal authorities have joined together to crack down on local builders. State officials are cracking down on subdivision contractors for building subdivisions without proper sewage systems. They are supported by the FHA, which will no longer approve loans for new construction in areas without proper sewers. One result has been the Belleville sewer program extension. In addition, some of the outlying subdivisions that do not wish to be annexed to the city are establishing their own sewage districts.

Central to the entire development of federal-state-local cooperation in these and other programs is the Belleville Chamber of Commerce. Despite the public position of the United States Chamber of Commerce regarding federal activities in the local community, the Belleville Chamber has a long record of involvement in support of federal and state cooperation with local agencies to further the goals of the civil community. After World War II, when the Belleville city government was at its lowest ebb, the Chamber acquired an old Army barracks which it moved to Belleville and managed as a veterans' housing project, a project that continued until 1953. During that period its management was entirely in the hands of the Chamber. In addition the Chamber of Commerce was involved, and very heavily involved indeed, in the creation of the Scott-Belleville Committee. The Chamber remains the administering agency within Belleville for the committee's activities.

Because the Chamber's membership and influence transcend the city limits of Belleville (even the businessmen of Swansea are members of the Belleville Chamber), it is highly useful for mobilizing support from the whole civil community. The Chamber handles most contacts with state and federal officials. It takes the lead in legislative issues, lobbying for the city and for the Air Force base with a freedom not available to formal government agencies and officials. The Chamber takes the lead in developing an annual highway program for Belleville for submission to the state. Indeed, the area plan committee of the Chamber has led in efforts to formulate plans for everything from airports to zoning and has been the gadfly in urging the formal government agencies to make use of federal-state and metropolitan area resources to advance along these and other lines.

Like most communities its size and smaller, Belleville presents a united front on most matters that require dealing with the state and federal governments. Indeed, the very character of its internal power structure extends its unity beyond the norm, to such a point that the state senator and the area's Congressmen jointly handle casework necessitating state and federal action. In the early 1960s they were in frequent contact with each other, exchanging between fifteen and twenty letters a week in an effort to aid Belleville and its citizens. Their relationship is characteristic of the approach taken by Belleville's leadership toward state and federal assistance. If it is available and they want to make use of it and it fits into the general ethos of the community, Bellevillians will unite to collaborate with both governments, regardless of ideological considerations. In turn, the "outside" aid they have received has been of crucial importance in the extension and improvement of local government services without compromising local interests in any perceivable way.

CHAPTER FIVE

THE

COURSE

OF

POSTWAR REFORM

The Calhoun Years

The fifteen years between 1947 and 1962 were years of major governmental reform in Belleville. The reform movement was built around the reorientation and expansion of Belleville's city government, but it grew so that it also affected most of the other public and quasi-public agencies in the civil community as well. In most of the other cities of the prairie, similar movements altered the structure of power locally. In Belleville the movement did not restructure the oligarchy so much as reaffirm its strength by giving it a chance to readjust to changing times and conditions. Since no major group in the civil community was excluded from a share in local political decision-making before 1949, no "revolution" was felt to be necessary by any significant number of local citizens. When it became apparent, however, that reform was needed, a reform movement developed from within the oligarchy and succeeded to a very great extent in achieving its limited goals.

In the years immediately preceding 1949, Belleville's city government had taken a turn away from the standards normally

---

Data for this chapter were obtained primarily from interviews with the individuals listed in Part 4 of Appendix B, p. 153.

imposed on local government by the civil community's ethical constitution. Observers of Belleville in those days summarize the situation succinctly: "The line between East St. Louis and Belleville had been let down." Apathy on the part of business and labor interests, perhaps bred of the Depression and war years, when public attention was focused on governments outside the civil community to the virtual exclusion of concern with local government, left local politics in the hands of those politicians who had maintained close contact with the county political organizations and were willing to accept the professional politicians' standards of political morality. Furthermore, the great expansion of Scott Air Force Base provided a market for the commodities merchandised (illegally) by those elements which provided much of the support for the county political organizations. These illegal activities, protected by the local authorities, were moved into Belleville proper. Gambling was rampant and slot machines were placed in taverns all over town. The tavern regulations were not enforced and liquor was sold to minors, both airmen and local civilians. The taverns became centers for prostitution which began to flourish in the city. According to local folklore, the notorious Shelton Gang, long active as the leading criminal group in southern Illinois, was involved in the introduction of this reign of vice.

While public tolerance of the situation continued for a number of years, and private indignation was not sufficient to overcome general community apathy, matters came to a head when the city's chief of police killed himself in his office rather than face a public scandal. After this public disgrace, the downtown businessmen appointed a citizens' committee, utilizing the Chamber of Commerce as the mechanism for creating it. The citizens' committee hired an attorney to investigate the local crime situation. His report was never made public, but as a result of his investigations, the citizens' committee made plans to institute far-reaching local reforms.

The first decision made by the committee was that Mayor Ernest Tieman, who had been elected in 1945, and had the reputation of being the most corrupt mayor in the city's history, had to be replaced. The committee, with the active help of the newspaper, convinced H. V. Calhoun, a local educator of forceful personality and a man known to be of the highest integrity, to run for mayor. In a three-way race which, on the surface, followed the typical pattern of slating and ticket-making in Belleville city politics, Calhoun won the biggest victory in the recent history of the city's mayoralty elections, perhaps in the entire history of Belleville. The roles of both the oligarchy and the voters were crucial. The politicians opposed Calhoun, the business community and the newspaper pulled out all stops to support him, and labor remained neutral. The voters, shocked by the public scandal, accepted the leadership of the pro-Calhoun forces.

The major emphasis in Calhoun's campaign was the promise that he would lead a reform administration to eliminate organized gambling and restore the barrier between Belleville and East St. Louis. Accordingly one of the first things he did after his election was to drive the gamblers out of the city, doing so with a thoroughness which set a pattern and which has prevented them from returning. In the process he devised the tactics currently in use to enforce the policy of opposing the East St. Louis element. It was he who introduced the practice of maintaining lists of undesirables who would be picked up on sight by the Belleville police. Calhoun's activities in the "clean-up" of the city probably won him more public approbation than any other accomplishments of his administration.

Calhoun was responsible for the reform of the police force, one of the primary goals of his administration and an essential part of his anti-gambling campaign. When he took office the police department was riddled with corruption. Most policemen apparently were being paid to allow gambling and prostitution to flourish. One of Calhoun's first acts was to have a civil service referendum submitted to the people which was passed the very year he took office and which put the police department under a merit system so extensive that it even included the police chief in the career service classification. The police force was increased from twenty-six to forty-one, which, while still considered too few by the present mayor and police chief, represented a considerable expansion for a city the size of Belleville.

Not only was the police force enlarged, but its personnel underwent a nearly complete turnover. Twenty-two of the twenty-six policemen on the force when Calhoun took office were replaced over the next five years. Calhoun did this by hiring a former St. Louis policeman, a "tough cop" with considerable ability and intelligence, to come in and reform the force. He has remained police chief and has developed a highly skilled department which works closely with the FBI and with the St. Louis Police Department in a partnership which has so far prevented the recurrence of the infiltration of criminal elements that preceded the Calhoun administration.

One result of the police reform has been the virtual elimination of prostitution within the city limits of Belleville. Whereas before 1949 prostitution was so rampant that the federal government used to check the city once a year for hygienic reasons to "protect" the servicemen stationed at the base, the federal inspectors have not been back since 1951. Another by-product of police reform has been better control of taverns and the sale of liquor. Tavern owners have been required to close on time since 1949 unless they receive special permission to stay open later for private parties. This system has been so well enforced that there were only eleven violations in 1961, in which only one involved a juvenile under sixteen. Not only that, but all the tavern owners must live in town; to the best of local officials' knowledge, all do.

The mayor also acted to raise the caliber of the civilian employees in the city government, to the extent possible under the prevailing "aldermanic courtesy" patronage system. This was considered necessary for the improvement of public services. Calhoun not only improved the city services then being provided, but also instituted free garbage collection, although this reform was subsequently modified by charging a fee to

TABLE 10

Illicit Activities in Belleville

Historical antecedents

old brewing town; beer gardens once popular;
heavy gambling in private clubs and taverns;
occasional flurries of prostitution

Contemporary manifestations

many taverns catering mainly to beer-drinkers;
gambling confined to some clubs after crackdown in recent years;
prostitution in city virtually nonexistent

Local attitude

casual attitude toward moderate (beer) drinking,
and continued interest in small-time gambling;
desire to keep prostitution out of town

Local government involvement

strong opposition to prostitution and threats by
East St. Louis crime syndicate to move into Belleville;
open gambling forbidden; more lenient
attitude toward gambling in clubs

cover part of the cost of collection. Mayor Calhoun was also responsible for the decision to build the new city hall. Construction was begun during his administration, though it was completed after he left office.

Once elected, Calhoun began to build an organization to support him and to make a series of reforms that changed the entire complexion of city government in Belleville. As a former school superintendent who embodied the mystique of the nonpartisan political administrator, he won the confidence of the local population. They gave him a level of support that is rarely given to professional politicians or even to businessmen-turned-politicians, but which is invariably reserved for chief school officers in our society. Mayor Calhoun and those associated with his administration were responsible either for implementing the new programs that made the reform movement meaningful, or for generating the ideas for new projects implemented by his successors (or being implemented now).

One of Calhoun's first steps in the building of his organization was to bring the Chamber of Commerce and organized labor together again. Over the years the two had developed a level of mutual antagonism, based on mutual misunderstanding, that prevented their effective communication and cooperation for the good of the community. Since the community's sociological constitution demands that all major elements be represented if the leadership is to take action, Calhoun's program depended on repairing this breach. His efforts cleared up the misunderstandings between the two to the extent that they have had no real trouble working together on public projects since then. As part of the bargain, the Chamber repudiated the United States Chamber of Commerce anti-union policies, and the local union leadership agreed that local incentives for economic development were necessary to provide the jobs no longer supplied by coal mining.

Once this was accomplished, the mayor could involve both elements in the development of a practical program of collaboration in the interest of Belleville's citizens. Mayor Calhoun's success in building a political structure which embraced the principles of his reform movement has been responsible for preserving the achievements of that movement since his departure from the scene.

Another problem the reformers tackled early in Calhoun's administration was industrial development. Calhoun himself had to do little to stimulate interest along this line. All that was necessary was to lend his support to the Chamber of Commerce. With the impetus of the mayor's support behind it, the Chamber, in cooperation with the Southern Railway System and the Illinois Power Company (both of which are interested in Belleville's economic growth because of Belleville's position in their respective territories) has attempted to bring new industry to town. In conjunction with other local business and manufacturing concerns, they developed three industrial development corporations: (1) the Belleville Industrial Development Corporation, whose job it is to convince new industries to locate in the community; (2) Belleville's New Industry Incorporated, nominally a profit-making investment company standing ready to invest in the provision of facilities to lease new industries, which was capitalized by the investment of the local merchants and even the labor unions; and (3) the Belleville Industrial Development Fund, another labor-management project (created in 1956, somewhat later than the first two).

As of 1962 the industrial development program had not succeeded in capturing any major new industry. The line of advancing industrialization on the metropolitan frontier, which has followed behind the line of residential suburbanization in the Madison-St. Clair Counties area, had yet to reach Belleville though it appeared about to do so. What local efforts did accomplish, in light of this debilitating reality, was to encourage the expansion of existing local industries to take up some of the slack in the local labor market. In addition, the Chamber of Commerce began promoting joint business-agricultural programs to bring the farmers into Belleville to shop and to use the city's services. This too added to the development of the local economy, although in a considerably smaller way.

Calhoun's interest in the Chamber of Commerce led to the development of a partnership between the Chamber and the city council which had also been lacking, partly because the heavily labor-influenced council had shared labor's distrust of the Chamber. Calhoun evidently realized that the Chamber could mobilize the talent needed to provide the type of advanced planning effort the city lacked and so desperately needed, but which was not available among the men of limited imagination on the city council. The first cooperative Chamber of Commerce-city council effort was the enactment of a new electrical code which became a good test case of the new cooperative spirit, involving as it did the regulation of the activities of a powerful local union. The spadework for the code was done by the Chamber of Commerce through one of its committees. The council, after holding hearings, enacted the code as a city ordinance.

Calhoun then began to develop a community planning program, a radical innovation in a city with no public planning programs of any kind, which traditionally had opposed all such activities as being government encroachment on individual freedom. As part of his planning effort, Calhoun revived the Planning Commission, which had been created by the previous administration primarily as a symbolic act (to show the world that Belleville was "up to date") and which had never been allowed to develop as an active body. Since "planning" was in principle anathema locally, and even limited comprehensive planning was opposed, Calhoun began to effectuate his planning goals piecemeal. He secured passage of a subdivision control ordinance, also with the cooperation of the Chamber. This provided the Chamber with the opportunity to create an area plan committee, a group composed of the supporters of planning, which was independent of the city and could act as a gadfly on behalf of planning programs. Calhoun tried to get a zoning ordinance enacted, but his efforts were too far ahead of the popular feeling and he failed, though he did initiate the effort that was kept alive over the years to bear fruit in the 1960s.

Calhoun instituted traffic control planning, first through a local study and then through a larger study conducted by Northwestern University. The plans that emerged from the two studies became the basis for a system of one-way streets which Calhoun instituted, as well as for a number of other proposals for traffic control, some of which have since been enacted.

Mayor Calhoun also tackled the parking problem. With the cooperation of the downtown businessmen, who provided much of the money, off-street parking lots were built. This issue became one of the few programmatic areas in which the downtown businessmen found themselves involved in a serious internal struggle. They could not agree among themselves on the location of the six parking lots to be built. The final location of the five city-owned lots is indicative of the relative political influence of the downtown businessmen. For example, the First National Bank was particularly active in the development of off-street parking and has a choice parking lot next door. The Citizens' Traffic Committee created by Calhoun remains as a continuing body, dedicated to the ongoing examination of the problems of parking and traffic.

Calhoun also initiated the sewer expansion program. The citizens' committee which he had activated handled the adoption of the sewer plan. That committee, which included the prime movers among the businessmen, with labor representation as well, sold the plan to the public, prevented the referendum, handled the issuance of $3,000,000 in bonds, and began negotiations with the federal government which culminated in the receipt of a $25,000 loan for planning the project, plus $45,000 for the first section to be constructed. As the sewer expansion program has developed since Calhoun's day, it has provided sewers for areas within the city which had none, particularly those annexed since 1949.

One of the major contributions of the Calhoun reform was the initiation of a policy of large-scale annexation of suburban areas, which has brought about a major increase in Belleville's land area. With the advice and consent of the business community, the mayor instituted the policy which was formally adopted by the city council that no city services would be provided to areas outside the city limits unless they agree to annexation. This led to twelve years of extensive annexation which has incorporated most of the newly settled fringe areas into the city of Belleville. While the newly annexed areas have required the expenditure of city funds to bring the level of their urban services up to urban standards, their inclusion within the city has prevented the development of serious suburban fringe problems found in so many other metropolitan communities.

Finally, Calhoun secured passage of legislation to redistrict the city's wards and precincts, thus bringing them in line with the population changes which had occurred as a result of the migrations of the post-World War II period. The new apportionment favored the better income districts, at the expense of older neighborhoods. While this did not change the balance of political power appreciably, it did solidify Calhoun's position by allowing those interested in reform to obtain better representation in political affairs and on the city council. Calhoun was able to do this because his ticket controlled the township as well as the city.

Calhoun was reelected for a second term in 1953, but only with some difficulty. His first four years had been so successful that his supporters had become apathetic. Following the typical pattern of business reform movements, the voters were interested in "throwing the rascals out" and putting an honest, efficient administrator in office, in the hope that they would then be able to retire from active concern with political matters. Of course what happened is that the opponents of reform, mostly professional politicians who remain active in politics year in and year out, rallied to oppose the mayor at the polls, while the mayor's supporters became overconfident and politically lax. Calhoun managed to win only because he had had the foresight to put together enough of an organization of his own to secure reelection. But he lost his majority in the council and was forced to continue his reform movement at a considerably slower pace.

Continuing Reform in the Post-Calhoun Years

In 1957 Calhoun decided not to run again, as it had become apparent that it would be difficult for him to win a third term. Active reform had apparently run its course in Belleville. Without Calhoun as a candidate to unite them, the three pillars of the oligarchy fell apart and three candidates were nominated for the office of mayor to succeed him. A majority of the prime movers of the business community united behind a local business leader, the owner of one of the metropolitan bus companies, who earnestly sought the office and used his influence to obtain business endorsement. The reformers, feeling that they needed to continue active reform, nominated a candidate of their own. Organized labor nominated a third candidate. Their candidate, Jerome J. Munie, was elected, much to the displeasure of the reformers and the businessmen who, while believing him to be honest, distrusted him because he was a former county politician.

The most important aspect of the 1957 mayoralty race was that all three candidates were men of exceptional integrity and ability. Whatever the decline of interest in active reform, it did not display itself in a desire to return to the old system. Calhoun had used his two terms to eliminate successfully any active opposition dominated by the "old pros," so that the only acceptable candidates were men committed to maintaining or extending his achievements. Munie had an exceptional record for a St. Clair County politician. He had been county sheriff some years earlier and was reputed to have been one of the two honest sheriffs in the history of St. Clair County. Between his term as sheriff and his election as mayor of Belleville, Munie had been a reform warden at the Menard State Penitentiary and had built a considerable reputation as a modern penologist.

Despite the trepidations of the businessmen and the reformers, Mayor Munie continued the policies of his predecessor and continued to advance the cause of reform, although his administration leaned slightly more toward labor than had the previous administration. Munie brought the off-street parking program to completion. He also brought the liquor control program a step further by encouraging the adoption of a license limit. An ordinance in 1957 provided for one liquor license to be issued for every five hundred people in the city. This meant that ideally there should be only eighty taverns in Belleville. When the license ordinance was passed there were 117. By 1962, the number had been reduced to 106 and was being further reduced by retiring licenses as individual taverns went out of business. In point of fact, the license limit measure was sponsored by the tavern owners' association, which, getting into the spirit of reform and realizing that it could benefit its members, promoted the measure to limit competition.

Mayor Munie also attempted to advance the course of planning in Belleville. He appointed the city's first urban renewal commission. This was the commission which, while consisting of a good representation from the oligarchy, ran afoul of public opinion before it could begin to function properly and had to desist from attempting any major urban-renewal activity.

Slightly more than halfway through his term, Mayor Munie became quite ill and was forced virtually to vacate his position. It was at that point that Charles Nichols, then the senior alderman on the city council, became acting mayor. It was the reputation which he built during the period of his acting mayoralty that gave him the nomination in 1961. Nichols won the support of the *News Democrat* by refusing to accept a bribe from a parking meter company and by reporting the offer to the press. After that incident, the publisher of the newspaper decided that Nichols would be the best candidate to maintain the reform movement. He promoted Nichols' candidacy and saw to it that Nichols was accepted by the other elements of the oligarchy. Since Nichols was a Republican at the time, the local representatives of the Republican Party were quite willing to accept him. Because he was a man of proven responsibility, the business community was also happy with him; because he was a leader in the teachers' union, organized labor was quite pleased with his selection; and, because he was a functioning alderman, the city hall politicians knew him and appreciated his talents. He won by a very impressive margin— 8,000 to 3,500.

Mayor Nichols did indeed continue the reform movement. Of his own volition, he became the first full-time mayor of Belleville, feeling that the mayor's salary, recently raised to $7,000, was sufficient to support him and his family and that the city's business required a full-time administrator. In general, Nichols continued the Calhoun program. He was responsible for the actual implementation of the sewer plan. He also completed the redistricting begun under Calhoun. In 1962 he was in the process of completing action on the adoption of a zoning ordinance.

Nichols added a new dimension to the planning program by beginning to enforce the health ordinance under which the city may demolish unsafe buildings. This is very difficult under Illinois law. Demolition orders must be implemented very slowly. Nichols decided to concentrate on spot demolition rather than to attempt a major renewal project at that time, on the grounds that there was too much that had to be done in the community before urban renewal could be tried. The urban renewal committee was reactivated under his administration, partly because one or two of the leaders of the business élite were interested in urban renewal, and the Southern Illinois University people were pressuring the city to do something about deteriorating neighborhoods.

Any discussion of urban renewal in Belleville is bound to generate tremendous public reaction in opposition. The public has been convinced that urban renewal is synonymous with public housing, which to them means "socialism" and Negroes. Since the exclusion of Negroes is a major preoccupation of Bellevillians, anything that even hints that Negroes might gain an entrance into the city is resisted forcefully. Therefore any urban rehabilitation program in Belleville had to be a conservation, rather than a clearance, program.

Among the new projects initiated by Mayor Nichols was the Richland Creek flood control project. Nichols became interested in the project because constituents in the Richland Creek area began making a fuss at city hall every time they were flooded out. He had to take the lead because the business community, which is not affected by the flooding, was somewhat less than concerned about implementing a major project of this nature unless it would cost the city little or no money. Many of the business leaders felt that the area should be evacuated and turned into parkland rather than spend the large sums required to safeguard it against floods. Objectively, they had a good case. However, since the mayor had the support of the city council, which was also getting pressure from its "wet" constituents and was likely to gain the support of labor (some of whose people were affected by the flooding), the project began to move into the active stage, held up only by the need to obtain state funds to match the federal contribution. Under these conditions, the business leadership indicated that it would not stand in the way. In fact, it was one of the leading business-men who suggested to the mayor that he turn to the state for the funds needed for the local share to match the federal grant.

Mayor Nichols altered the previous policy of the reform movement in one way by stopping the major annexation pro-gram. He was convinced that most of the city's major problems had been caused by bringing in semi-developed areas which required extensive investment of city funds to bring them up to Belleville's level. Since the city was in a very poor financial condition, the mayor felt it could not afford to take in any more large areas, then have to provide for their development. So he instituted a policy of annexing new territories by individual lot only, at the city's convenience.

A major set-to in the Nichols' administration, illustrative of Belleville's tenuous independence and the efforts made to pre-serve it, was the problem of securing payment of personal prop-erty taxes by city employees. Though legally bound to pay, city employees were allowed, by local custom, to avoid that burden. The mayor's effort to collect the taxes provided the grounds for "Boss" Fields' only intervention into city affairs since Nichols' election. Nichols instructed all city employees to pay their taxes or risk being fired. Fields, through his politi-cal followers among the precinct committeemen in Belleville, let it be known that this was not necessary. After a considerable conflict, during which he again threatened to fire all those who did not pay, Nichols won.

In seeking to deal with the city's fiscal crisis, Nichols' admin-istration subsequently became involved in the problem of per-sonal property tax collections in St. Clair County as a whole, thereby extending reform in yet another direction. Until recently, St. Clair County did not collect personal property taxes, though it was legally bound to do so by state law. This had the effect of depriving the civil divisions of the county of a major source of revenue. Belleville's oligarchy, under the leadership of Mayor Nichols, fought for the collection of the taxes because the city needed the money. They were opposed by the most powerful political figure in the county and his organization. By obtaining state intervention in the matter, the pro-tax collection forces turned the tide in their direction early in 1962.

Reforming the Whole Civil Community

One measure of the unity of the civil community is the manner in which the reform movement spread beyond the confines of the city limits of Belleville proper. In one way or another, the other governments in the civil community also responded to the pressures for change which helped generate municipal reform in Belleville.

Even before the great burst of energy that marked the reform movement, Bellevillians voted to establish a public junior college, which has come to be a center for training skilled workers for new job markets. The other schools, pressured by the rise in enrollment both from migration into the community and from the increased local birthrate, have had to float bond issue after bond issue to extend their facilities. For the most part, efforts to gain voter approval for the bond issues have been successful in the past despite a strong reluctance in the community to spend money for public purposes, no matter what the public purposes were. Recently, however, the schools have been running into greater difficulty in acquiring new funds to continue their necessary expansion programs.

Not only have the schools enlarged their capacities, but they have upgraded their facilities. The architecture of Belleville's new school buildings is notable even in a day of imaginative school architecture. It combines money-saving features with attractiveness and a high degree of utility. In general the school systems have been endeavoring to adjust their curricula to the changes in community and society, particularly since 1957.

The city's recreation department has also expanded its program since 1949. A new park has been added under the general jurisdiction of the recreation director. Fifty-five and a half acres in area, Citizens' Park, as it is called, was financed by private donations. The recreation director, in cooperation with the Chamber of Commerce and the young people who participate in the recreation program, raised the money to buy land and secured the donation of work and equipment. They have continued to raise money for improvements and the annual maintenance cost, and have produced the only addition to the city's park system in a generation. The park itself is located outside the city limits and the city government is not involved directly in its development, except through the recreation director.

Other private activities leading to public improvement have also developed in the past thirteen years. The Chamber of Commerce, the downtown businessmen, and the women's clubs have tried to develop a program for esthetic improvement of the central business district and the various residential sections, ranging from a "clean-up, paint-up, fix-up" campaign to an attempt at beautification of the downtown streets and store fronts. This program has met with mixed results, as all such private beautification programs do. It does have a certain amount of legal reinforcement through a city ordinance requiring people to cut the weeds in their yards. The ordinance is enforced with some regularity because those interested in civic beautification put pressure on city officials to do so. As usual, pressure counts, no matter what its source. Similar improvements have been fostered in the realm of governmental and public nongovernmental social welfare services, ranging from food distribution programs to a new YMCA building. A concert and guest artist series has been inaugurated to upgrade the cultural facilities of the civil community, and is advertised as a means of attracting desirable industry. Private construction of public facilities from parking lots to elegant restaurants to new motels has been important in maintaining the viability of the central business district. In general, it may be said that the political aspects of reform have been tied in with the overall dynamics of change in an area that is being affected by numerous changes, many of which are beyond its control.

The Future of Local Reform

After over twelve years of reform Belleville had not changed its basic outlook even as it tried to adapt that outlook to changing times and conditions. At the same time, it appears that the basic premises of reform did indeed make a permanent impression on the civil community, assisted by Belleville's background, its general inclination to support honest government, and the strength of the reform movement since 1949. Consequently by 1962 it was very unlikely that there would be any relapse into pre-1949 conditions. This was made doubly likely by virtue of the strength of the representative oligarchy, all of whose elements appeared to be committed to the maintenance of reform in this sense.

Belleville spent the late 1950s and the 1960s trying to assimilate reform with as little change as possible. While it mobilized excellent cadres of civil and political leaders, it did not acquire professional leadership for the civil community of the kind which may be needed to maintain the newly established standards of local services. There was no effort to change the form of city government, because there was really no need to change it; but neither was there any serious effort to improve the city's financial condition, which did need improvement desperately.

Many of the most important administrative improvements have been of an ad hoc nature. Whether future mayors will have the administrative competence of Mayor Nichols and whether they will be willing to devote full time to the job is necessarily uncertain. Much of the city's future development will depend on what happens in this regard, since there are no professional generalists who can step in to maintain the pace regardless of changes among the elected officeholders. In the meantime Belleville, unlike most of its sister cities, has been able to sustain a reform movement beyond the usual four to six years of citizen interest.

CHAPTER SIX

OLIGARCHY AND REFORM
IN
BELLEVILLE

In the mid-1960s Belleville was a civil community that had responded to the challenges of the metropolitan frontier in a manner intended to accommodate both the values of its citizens and the demands of the times. It seems to have done so in a reasonably appropriate and effective manner. Such a statement must be made cautiously; nevertheless, it is made with some conviction as to its accuracy. Belleville is not an ideal polity, nor is it necessarily a model for other civil communities. Moreover, it is particularly difficult to judge how well a polity responds to the challenges before it until long after those challenges have passed. Any judgment made now must necessarily be tentative, particularly in light of the changes that have taken place in American society since the early 1960s.

This study of Belleville was completed as the metropolitan frontier, or at least its first phase, reached its climax nationally. The administration of President Kennedy, who was elected on the basis of an appeal to Americans to recognize the existence of the "New Frontier," marked the beginning of this generation's response to the problems generated by that frontier on a national scale. In this respect, the Kennedy administration, and the Johnson administration even more so, continued the tradition of generational responses to the challenges which have confronted each generation in American history, with the added fillip of having to respond to an entirely new frontier stage as well.

At the same time, the response to the frontier came precisely as the first phase of the frontier had reached its conclusion. Since the mid-1960s Americans, nationally and locally, have had to deal with the backlash of the frontier, with the human displacement and social disorganization it has caused, together with its benefits, with the problems involving black migrants to the urban ghettos and those involving the children of white migrants in the suburbs. The ghetto and the suburb are both products of the metropolitan frontier. The ghetto represents the opening which that frontier provided the blacks to enter into the new industrial society and leave their rural base behind. The suburb represents the cutting edge of the settlement pattern of the metropolitan frontier as a whole.

No one needs to document the fact that the children of the urban ghetto reflect social disorganization. While we normally think of the suburbs as being places of tranquility, in fact, their tranquility is often simply superficial precisely because they are (or have been) frontier areas. Psychologically and physically they are (or have been) places of upheaval, of uprooting and movement, of unanticipated social change; so it is not surprising that the children of the suburbs should reflect that discomfiture.

Belleville has been on the periphery of both aspects of the backlash, but it has not fully escaped either in the years since the completion of this study. The questions that have arisen since 1965 fit into a different context and must be dealt with at another time. Here we have focused on a civil community's response to the salad days of the third great frontier in American history, and it is that response which must be evaluated in this brief conclusion.

We must begin by reemphasizing that local politics in urban America is not synonymous with the politics of cities. The overlapping character of the many governmental institutions in any particular locality requires a definition of political community that is not necessarily demarcated by any specific political boundary. Local politics, then, is the politics of the civil community.

The Belleville civil community enjoys a vast array of institutions which have developed since the nineteenth century to help meet the increasing number of public problems with which it has had to deal. In dealing with these problems the civil community has relied on governmental and nongovernmental institutions. Historically there has been a shift from nongovernmental to governmental institutions in the provision of public services desired by its citizenry. Nevertheless, governmental institutions have been used only as a last resort. This hesitancy to use the power of government even to achieve public purposes is part and parcel of the general American political culture. It is, however, particularly a feature of the Belleville political subculture, which is an amalgam of traditionalistic and individualistic elements, leaning toward the latter subcultural strain. Reluctance to call upon government has placed important limitations on what local government is able to do, even in the period of intensive political response that has been discussed in this book.

The institutional framework for Belleville's politics was built up, as it were, over the course of a century and a half, without any overall plan, but in response to locally perceived needs and occasional outside pressures, conditioned by the community's fundamental political cleavages and power relationships. Indeed, to understand the community's political behavior, it is necessary to understand these fundamental cleavages and relationships and to distinguish them from transient and passing ones. As we have seen, the basis of cleavage in Belleville is cultural as much as it is economic. In this respect Belleville is no different than most communities in the greater West.

Belleville, a civil community economically more equalitarian than most, has fewer extremes of rich or poor because of the particular historical and geographic circumstances that have influenced its development. Consequently it may have been even more affected by cultural cleavages than its sisters. The cleavages have taken two forms. The first developed out of the different streams of migration coming into the community. It was based essentially on the ethnic differences that dominated the civil community in the nineteenth century. The second and present cleavage is based on the socio-religious ties that have grown out of the ethnic communities after the more overt ethnic differences disappeared in the process of Americanization. The latter ties, however, have been institutionalized far more than the former ever were, because they are part and parcel of the American scene and not simply transient phenomena of pioneering generations.

Belleville differs from many of its sister communities in the way in which power has been organized around these political cleavages. Its particular mode of organization of power has been characterized as a representative oligarchy, based on three great "pillars"—the business community, the labor unions, and the politicians-cum-public officials. Each pillar represents a particular constituency and exerts its power by virtue of its general acceptance as the authoritative representative of that constituency. Together the three pillars exercise power because they are considered the authoritative representatives of the civil community as a whole. This is evident, among other ways, in the manner in which the community will withdraw its support from the oligarchy when it is no longer considered representative on a particular issue. Several examples of this were cited earlier.

It is this quality of representativeness that has helped the oligarchy survive and even thrive over 150 years of the community's history. No doubt the relatively moderate political climate which seems to have pervaded Belleville from the first, combined with the community's relatively equalitarian socioeconomic base and supported by the community's nearly unanimous concern for keeping itself separate from East St. Louis and its American Bottoms neighbors, has strengthened the ability of the representative oligarchy to survive. What is also clear is that the oligarchy has made the periodic adaptations necessary to keep it representative. The record of the fifteen years from the late 1940s to the early 1960s, during which a major political reform movement was mounted through the oligarchy and succeeded in reshaping the direction of the ruling elements in the community, is the most recent case in point.

In a community like Belleville, which for cultural reasons likes orderly arrangements, a representative oligarchy has proved to be most functional. Over and over, Bellevillians told the author that Belleville is an orderly community because of its German background. Be that as it may, the local population strongly believes that this is the case, and the long, uninterrupted history of the representative oligarchy lends credence to their belief.

In sum, we have tried to indicate how public policy in Belleville is, to a considerable extent, a function of the institutions of the civil community, the social and cultural character of the polity, and the locally felt need to define the community in relation to the outside world. Yet with all these factors accounted for, the result is not predetermined. The development of political coalitions is dependent on the activities of the political leadership, the representatives of the three "pillars," who can either work cooperatively or engage in conflict—sometimes minor, sometimes prolonged, occasionally bitter. If the larger forces help shape them, their decisions are yet open ones, open to respond to the currents of the day, to each other, and to transient pressures. If cooperation seems to be best achieved by emphasizing Belleville's distinctive character as a civil community, in contrast to East St. Louis and its environs (the undesirable outside enemy), then that too has its political uses and must be recognized in that context.

As we try to assess the relationship between formal governmental structures, the informal structure of power, and the capacity of the civil community to deal with its problems, we are entitled to ask some very direct questions. Who has gained and who has lost from the organizational workings of the community's political arrangements? What has been achieved and what has been sacrificed, given Belleville's set of governing institutions and the politics that animate them?

The author believes that it can fairly be said—as of 1962—that no one in particular gained or lost much more than anyone else in the civil community, with two possible exceptions: the small Negro population has failed to gain at all and the business community has gained something of an extra advantage over the years. The Negro community has failed to gain in the sense that it has remained a small, excluded community, with no share in the governing of Belleville and no representation in the power system. No doubt because they still "knew their place," as defined by the white community, the Negroes exhibited no political demands, so there was no question of dealing with them politically. This is highly significant, especially in light of what has happened nationally and in the St. Louis metropolitan region since the early 1960s.

The business community has probably gained somewhat more than any group, although not greatly. Because the city's leaders have defined the civil community's concerns as being almost identical with the concerns of the downtown businessmen, they have stood to gain on most decisions. At the same time, it is apparent from the issues on which they were defeated that they were not given anything like a blank check. They had to compete for their gains, just like everyone else, but the nature of their interest, given the orientation of civil communities such as Belleville, puts them right in the mainstream of the culturally conditioned views about what is good for the local community, views that tend to dominate local leaders no matter what positions they occupy. If the strengthening of the central business district is identified with what is good for Belleville, it is no wonder that the business community stands to gain.

Among the other interests in the community, there are no great gainers and no great losers, because politically the various interests have been content to protect their respective "games." In his very suggestive article, "Local Government as an Ecology of Games," Norton Long has suggested that a community's political system really has to do with the interlinkages among various games being played by the various interests, some of which overlap considerably and some of which are generally fairly well separated, although never entirely so. It is useful to apply this approach to Belleville. Each of the various interests in the community has its own games. They worry first and foremost about protecting those games, and insofar as local political institutions affect them, they will worry about local political institutions. Beyond that, they are relatively unconcerned about what goes on in local politics.

Since the games of the business community tend to overlap the local political system most extensively, businessmen tend to be most heavily involved in policy problems. While the local politician's game may seem to be more thoroughly identical with the local political game, in fact it is identical in a very narrow way, so that politicians are able to structure their participation so as to protect themselves by being a little bit in everything, but only as much as necessary to retain their position as brokers. This the representative oligarchy in Belleville assures them, so they ask for no more.

More peripheral, and more easily taken care of, are the games of the various socio-religious groups. The Fundamentalists, for example, play an almost totally apolitical game, hence they make the fewest demands on the political system. Consequently, they cannot be said to be losers, even though they seem to gain almost nothing. From time to time, the Fundamentalists lose on a particular issue that affects them. For example, they may have to move out of their houses in the lowlands for the flood control project. But these events are too rare to stimulate them to reevaluate their own attitude toward politics.

Labor in Belleville seems to be so thoroughly identified with middle-class aspirations and interests—indeed, with the kind of artisanship that brings economic reward only as long as the central business district remains economically healthy—that it too does not feel the need to bring its games into conflict with the other political games very often. Tax issues probably threaten Belleville's workingmen and their families the most and on those issues their own demands for better services, modest as they may be, tend to cancel out the question of winning and losing, or at least to make it far more complex.

In all these areas the existence of the representative oligarchy provides a means for regulating the interaction among the various games and players and, in most cases, for smoothing out difficulties that arise among them. Indeed, it is only when the leadership of the pillars cannot smooth out the difficulties that the oligarchy is bypassed. Usually in such cases, the largest element in the public wins its point, even in opposition to its own leaders.

In this connection the very multiplicity of institutions and the apparently irrational pattern of allocating functions among them provides an institutional base that allows the various games to go on with the least amount of conflict. In large part, this is because the multiplicity of specialized institutions and the division between governmental and nongovernmental institutions virtually eliminate the necessity for any single institution to have to make hard choices among the various interests. This is certainly one of the reasons why Americans in all communities—indeed, on all planes of government—have tended to want to diffuse power. As long as the resources that enable Americans to tolerate a certain amount of "duplication" and "inefficiency" are there, from a strictly economic standpoint, the multiplication of institutions is a cheap way of purchasing political harmony while at the same time protecting the varied interests in the nation and in its civil communities.

Why should people who love parks more than anything have to fight every day of the week with people who want better roads more than anything? It is enough that they must clash when a road threatens a park. A separate park jurisdiction with a separate policy-making body and perhaps a separate tax levy can make its decisions while the city council, functioning as a road commission with its own tax base, can make its decisions, thereby minimizing the need to vacillate at every turn between conflicting goals. Even if those who argue, often persuasively, that the complexity of society today makes this wasteful have a point, their point must be judged in terms of the likely political and social consequences of generating intense day-to-day conflict by eliminating such "wasteful duplication." By its very intensity, such conflict will not necessarily produce better results than the system of diffusion of responsibility.

Perhaps herein lies the lesson that this civil community and other "Bellevilles" in the contemporary United States can teach all of us: namely, how to manage conflict and produce consensus under conditions that promise at least a rough equity treatment for all concerned in light of their values and expectations as citizens.

APPENDIX A

THE
METHOD
OF
EXPLORATION

The overall study of medium-size civil communities, the results of which are partially reported in this book, was conducted over approximately four years (preparation for the field work was begun in October 1959; field work was begun in January 1960 and concluded in June 1963), primarily by one trained political scientist (the author), assisted in his office by various graduate and undergraduate research assistants, never more than one at a time. Consequently this study represents such limitations as are inherent in work done by one human being, as well as the advantage of a high level of control over comparability of perception, field-work techniques, and data analysis. Continued consultation and collaboration with colleagues, some of whom had studied or were studying some of the same metropolitan areas for other purposes, was intended to overcome some of the possible deficiencies of a one-man project. Nevertheless, it is clear to the author that some limitations connected with this fact remain.

Because one man was studying ten metropolitan areas in less than four years (together with other responsibilities which prevented him from devoting full time to this project), it was manifestly impossible to come to know any of the ten areas as intimately as have many of the participant observers among the

This appendix is adapted from *Cities of the Prairie.*

sociologists and anthropologists who have devoted full time to participant observation in single communities for a year or more, although the author's residence was in Champaign-Urbana for the entire period and longer, during which time he systematically observed local politics there. In fact, an average of three months was spent on each metropolitan area, divided as follows: two to four weeks of preparation in the office prior to going into the field (reviewing background data and existing research on the community, selecting the particular issues and cases to be studied in light of the overall scheme, refining the questions to be asked, and acquiring the names of people to interview); intensive field work in the metropolitan area itself of from eight days to seven weeks, depending on the number and size of the central cities in each metropolitan area, and based on approximately two weeks per central city; approximately five weeks spent after returning from the field in reviewing and digesting the interview transcripts and the collected documentary material and ordering it so as to present a socio-political profile of each metropolitan area; and an additional two to four weeks of library research to fill in needed historical background and to complete other necessary follow-up work. During this entire process, continued research and reading was done on the general background of the entire complex of civil communities considered in the overall study.

The author discovered, after two trial runs, that the period of approximately two weeks per central city would enable him to gather as much information as possible short of spending a year in residence as a participant observer in each civil community. The surface and immediate subsurface information, which leads to a good general outline of community politics, plus in-depth information for one or more case studies, could be obtained through intensive interviewing and gathering of documentary materials in that period of time, while extensions short of a year yielded diminishing returns. A year or thereabouts of virtually single-minded study in each community would be necessary to penetrate into the nuances of its politics. This field-work pattern was adhered to in six of the metropolitan areas and in one city of the seventh. The complexity of the Madison-St. Clair Counties area would have required three months of field work under the formula. Fortunately, by cooperating with two political scientists of the Institute of Public Administration and Metropolitan

Affairs at Southern Illinois University, it was possible to make use of their field work, allowing the author to concentrate on Belleville.

The research program undertaken in this fashion was predicated on the feasibility of combining (1) selective interviewing of political and community actives in depth; (2) limited on-the-spot observation of events; (3) extensive review of the local press; (4) utilization of other relevant studies of the ten metropolitan areas or their component civil communities; (5) collection of basic socio-economic data prepared for each metropolitan area by other agencies; (6) review of relevant historical materials available; (7) compilation of significant election data, with judicious analysis based on reasonably rigorous hypotheses; and (8) systematic, unobtrusive observation of all visible aspects of the civil community.

From twenty to seventy people were interviewed in each civil community, with interviews ranging in length from thirty minutes to fifteen hours (over several days). Those interviewed were selected from a list which included (1) all locally elected officials; (2) appointed heads of government and major government agencies in the area; (3) major political leaders; (4) major civic leaders; (5) officers and executives of civic associations, chambers of commerce, and the like; (6) representatives of the local press and mass media; (7) major business, professional, and industrial leaders; and (8) people suggested by others interviewed as particularly good sources of information.

No list was covered exhaustively, both because of time limitations and because a number of the people simply were unavailable during the period of field work in each area. The author believes, however, that the distribution was wide enough to be representative of the categories on the list and that the interviewees were generally astute enough to have provided him with information as detailed and accurate as that available through survey research and other ostensibly "harder" data—and even more perceptive.

The author attended all public and private meetings of governmental bodies, political organizations, civic groups, chambers of commerce and business groups, and private gatherings of political actives held during his stay which were open to him. Even in the relatively short time available in each city, this was of substantial value for observing people who had been interviewed "in action" and for getting the "feel" of politics in the community.

It was also valuable as a starting point for re-interviewing participants after the meetings, usually in an informal setting, at which time the author was able to ask more pointed questions which, by tying in with the more general questions asked in the formal interview, served both as an addition to and a corroboration of the latter. Since access into even the most intimate meetings of a political or civic nature was rarely denied, this was a highly productive aspect of the field work.

All the newspapers published in each metropolitan area were intensively reviewed for the field-work period. This was coupled with a review of older material relevant to specific issues being examined in depth, such as council-manager referenda, and with interviews of editors, publishers, and reporters for elaboration on the published accounts. The newspapers were used as sources of information on matters directly political and for background on the metropolitan area as a whole. Of course, the mass media were studied as actors on the local scene, as well as chroniclers of it, particularly since, in more than one case, the character of the chronicles was directly related to the interests of the newspapers as actors.

Such studies—academic, quasi-academic, and reform-oriented—as existed for each of the metropolitan areas, few as they were, were examined critically and, where possible, the studies were discussed (and the data on which they were based reviewed) with those who had commissioned them or carried them out. Relatively few academic studies were available for the ten areas; even fewer were directly concerned with political phenomena. During the first year of research, Richard Robbins was engaged in a study of the effectiveness of local human relations commissions and allied bodies in many of the same cities; this was particularly useful in uncovering information pertaining to the Negro communities in those cities. The following year, Rondal G. Downing studied judicial politics in Illinois and included within his study the Madison-St. Clair Counties metropolitan area. His data helped confirm the author's analysis of the regional relationships within that metropolitan area as well as filling in gaps in our knowledge of a major area of political activity in the state of Illinois and its subdivisions. Finally, the continuing work of Seymour Mann and Eleanor Schwab at the East St. Louis campus of Southern Illinois University in studying the Madison-St. Clair

Counties area served to reinforce the author's work in the Belleville area in many ways.

Aside from these academic studies, the League of Women Voters chapters in most of the communities studied had prepared descriptions of the formal governmental systems of their communities of varying scope and quality, all of which were useful. Similar material, often with interesting appendages concerning the less formal processes of government, had been prepared by chambers of commerce in some of the cities studied for use in their practical politics courses. Public administration and planning studies were also of use in providing background information. None of the civil communities studied was without at least one of these. Often there were several, prepared over a forty-year period and valuable as historical as well as contemporary documents. All told, a reasonable body of this kind of literature, of varying quality, could be unearthed for almost every metropolitan area to supplement other forms of data-gathering.

Basic socio-economic data in a variety of forms were collected from the census reports, planning agencies, industrial development groups, private industry, chambers of commerce, and other state and federal sources. Many governmental and private agencies assemble statistical data on a wide variety of matters. These data were used as indicators of a similarly wide variety of patterns and trends in the civil community. Furthermore, standard publications such as city and telephone directories carry within them many implicit indicators of the same sort. Historical "indicators" taken from the records and from secondary sources available for each metropolitan area were examined as thoroughly as possible. Scholarly histories were used wherever they were available. Semi-scholarly and filio-pietistic histories of cities and counties were of particular use in tracing patterns over time, despite their obvious deficiencies. Some communities are fortunate in having active local historical societies with collections of documents and with members who themselves have written articles and papers on local history. In addition, city records and reports and general books and articles dealing with the areas in question were reviewed.

Voting returns for selected national, state and local elections and state and local referenda were assembled, with decreasing thoroughness, back to the earliest days of organized government in each metropolitan area. Significant gaps exist in the availability of voting data at the local level in the communities studied, limiting the extent of data analysis possible.

The author systematically observed the physical manifestations of life in each civil community along the lines subsequently set forth in *Unobtrusive Measures.** Street and land-use patterns; characteristics and distribution of business, residential, industrial, and recreational areas; architectural styles; public advertising; the character and availability of newspapers, magazines, and books; the quality of merchandise available in various kinds of stores; and many other such measures available through unobtrusive observation reveal much about the character, concerns, and underlying values that influence politics in each civil community.

Underlying these eight facets of community research was the outline and guide for studying the civil community since published separately in a revised edition by the Center for the Study of Federalism as *Studying the Civil Community* (Philadelphia, 1970).

---

*Eugene J. Webb, Donald T. Campbell, Richard D. Schwartz and Lee Sechrest, *Unobtrusive Measures* (Chicago: Rand McNally, 1966).

APPENDIX B

SELECTED
BIBLIOGRAPHY

Public Documents and Newspapers

Belleville *News Democrat* (and predecessors), some issues dating back to 1858.

Charter of the City of Belleville, 1867.

City Directory of Belleville, 1860 to present.

Constitution of the State of Illinois. Secretary of State of Illinois, Springfield, n. d.

Government in Illinois. Secretary of the State of Illinois, Springfield. (n.d.)

Illinois Blue Book, 1881-1967.

Proceedings of the Belleville City Council, 1894-1909.

Revised Ordinances of the City of Belleville Codifications: 1855, 1862, 1890, 1913, 1960.

Books and Articles

Ackerman, William K. *Early Illinois Railroads.* Chicago: Fergus Printing, 1884. Read before the Chicago Historical Society, February 20, 1883.

Allen, John W. *Legends and Lore of Southern Illinois.* Carbondale, Ill.: Southern Illinois University Press, 1963.

150

Althoff, Phillip and Samuel C. Patterson. "Political Activism in a Rural County." *Midwest Journal of Political Science,* vol. 10 (February 1966), pp. 39-151.

Bateman, Newton and Paul Selby, eds. *Historical Encyclopedia of Illinois,* vol. 1. Chicago: Munsell Publishing Company, 1916.

Beuckman, Frederic. *History of the Diocese of Belleville,* 1919.

Blair, George. *Cumulative Voting.* Urbana, Ill.: University of Illinois Press, 1960.

Calley, Charles C. *Pilot Study of Southern Illinois.* Carbondale, Ill.: Southern Illinois University Press, 1956.

Faith, Emil F. and Richard G. Browne. *Government and History of the State of Illinois.* Chicago: Mentzer, Bush, 1956.

Fisher, Glenn W. *Financing Illinois Government.* Urbana, Ill.: University of Illinois Press, 1960.

Gamberg, Herbert V. *A Working Paper on Urban Political Capabilities.* Urbana, Ill.: University of Illinois, Office of Community Development, March 1963. Mimeo.

Garvey, Neil F. *The Government and Administration of Illinois.* New York: Thomas Y. Crowell, 1958.

Gove, Samuel K., ed. *Illinois State Government: A Look Ahead.* Urbana, Ill.: University of Illinois Press, 1958.

———, *State and Local Government in Illinois: A Bibliography.* Urbana, Ill.: University of Illinois Press, 1953.

Gove, Samuel K. and Alvin I. Sokolow, eds. *1958 Supplement to State and Local Government in Illinois: A Bibliography.* Urbana, Ill.: University of Illinois Press, 1958.

Gove, Samuel K. and Gilbert Y. Steiner, *The Illinois Legislative Process. University of Illinois Bulletin,* 54:75. (1959).

Hirchcliffe, John. *Historical Review of Belleville,* 1870. *History of St. Clair County,* 1881.

Howards, Irving. *Selected Aspects of State Supervision Over Local Government in Illinois: A View of State-Local Relations.* Carbondale, Ill.: Southern Illinois Press, 1964.

Illinois Government. University of Illinois, Institute of Government and Public Affairs, August 1962.

Illinois: A Descriptive and Historical Guide. Originally compiled and written by the Federal Writers' Project for the State of Illinois. Chicago: A. C. McClurg, 1939 (revised 1946).

Journal of the Illinois State Historical Society. Emancipation Centennial Issue. Springfield, Ill. (Autumn 1963).

Journal of the State Historical Society of Illinois, 1921-1968.

Littlewood, Thomas B. *Bipartisan Coalition in Illinois.* Eagleton Institute Cases in Practical Politics, no. 22 (1960).

MacRae, Duncan, Jr. and James A. Meldrum. "Critical Elections in Illinois: 1888-1958," *American Political Science Review,* 54 (1960), 669-83.

Masters, Nicholas A., Robert H. Salisbury, and Thomas H. Eliot. *State Politics and Public Schools.* New York: Alfred A. Knopf, 1964.

Municipal Human Relations Councils, The Institute of Government and Public Affairs. *Illinois Government.* no. 6 (February 1960).

Nebelsick, A. L. *A History of Belleville.* (privately printed)

Nodger, Carl F. *Illinois Negro Historymakers.* Chicago: Emancipation Centennial Commission, 1964.

Pelekoudas, Lois M. *The Illinois Constitution.* Urbana, Ill.: University of Illinois Press, 1962.

———, ed. *Illinois Local Government.* Urbana, Ill.: University of Illinois Press, 1961.

———, ed. *Illinois Political Parties.* Urbana, Ill.: University of Illinois Press, 1960.

Petty, A. F. "The Economic Geography of Belleville." Unpublished Master's thesis, University of Illinois, Urbana, 1939.

Ranney, Austin. *Illinois Politics.* New York: New York University Press, 1960.

Reavis, W. C. "Survey Report of Belleville Township High School and Junior College," 1954 (unpublished)

Snider, Clyde F. and Irving Howards. *County Government in Illinois.* Carbondale, Ill.: Southern Illinois University Press, 1960.

Reports, Files, and Miscellaneous Publications

Belleville Chamber of Commerce, "Manufacturers and Utilities List." March 1962.

———. "Community Information Belleville, Illinois." 1961.

———. 'Statistics and Facts Concerning Belleville, Illinois." May 1962.

———. "Activities in Belleville." March 1962.

———. "1961 Progress Report, Belleville, Illinois." (n. d.)

———. "1961 List of Industrial Towns in the Belleville and St. Louis Area." (n. d.)

———. "Annual Report." 1960, 1961, 1962.

———. "Architects, Construction Contractors, Developers, and Related Services, Belleville, Illinois." (n. d.)

———. "Associations, Clubs, and Organizations." August 1961.

———. "Churches in Belleville." June 1960. Belleville Junior Chamber of Commerce. "Belleville, Illinois—Community Problems Survey, 1961-1962." 1962.

Council of Community Development. Report distributed to the members of Council of Community Development, January 24, 1961, by Dr. Merle R. Sumption, chairman of the Metropolitan Area School District Organization Committee. "A Study of Metropolitan Area School District Organization in Illinois, December 28, 1960."

Federal Reserve Bank of Chicago. *Annual Report.* 1959-1964.

Interviews

NOTE: A number of important interviews from the Belleville area have not been cited to preserve confidences. They are available in the files of the Institute of Government and Public Affairs of the University of Illinois and the Center for the Study of Federalism, Temple University.

Joe Adam, Reporter: Belleville *News-Democrat.*

R. G. Dabson, Belleville Chief of Police.

Alan Dixon, State Senator, St. Clair County.

Eugene Graves, Southern Illinois University Community Development Worker, East St. Louis.

Gene Hayes, Former St. Clair County Political Leader.

P. K. Johnson, City Attorney, Belleville.

Peter Kern, Publisher, Belleville *News-Democrat.*

Seymour Z. Mann, Director, Bureau of Public Administration and Metropolitan Affairs, S. I. U. Edwardsville Campus.

Devereaux H. Murphy, St. Clair County Highway Commissioner.

Charles E. Nichols, Mayor of Belleville.

P. C. Otwell, Attorney, Former Democratic City Chairman.

Clifford Peake, Belleville Chamber of Commerce Manager.

Al Pierce, Belleville Town Auditor, Former Constable.

Leroy Roberts, Office Manager for Belleville Township.

Walter Ryan, Realtor, Civic Leader.

John Thompson, City Engineer, Belleville.

P. K. Wellinghausen, Former State Representative, Civic Leader.

Jack Wellinghoff, President, Belleville-St. Louis Coach Co.

Gene Widman, Attorney, Former Democratic City Chairman.

INDEX

Agricultural implements, manufacture of, 38
Air facilities, of Saint Louis, 40–41
Airport, municipal, campaign for, 84–85, 87
Aldermen, 76, 94, 96
American Association of State Highway Officials, 109
American Bottoms, 21–22, 38, 138–39; domination of local politics by organizations in, 75; immigrants from, 69–70; industrialization of, and partisan politics, 72, 75; isolation from, 68; Negroes in, 68; organized crime in, 69
American Federation of Labor (AFL), 42
Anglo-Canadian cultural stream, 10–11
Annexation of suburban areas, 126, 131
Architecture: contemporary American suburban, 26; German, 25–26; of schools, 132; Southern, 24, 26
Autocracy: and oligarchy, 79; as political control, 78

Backlash, 136

Bankers: in business community, 86–87; as Protestants, 89
Banks: Belleville National Bank, 41; Belleville Savings Bank, 41; First National Bank of Belleville, 41, 86, 125–26; Saint Clair National Bank, 41
Baptist: Church, 33; early Southern, congregation, 28
Beer, 37. *See also* Breweries.
Belle Valley (common school) District, 52, 106
Belleville Chamber of Commerce, 54–55, 83, 85; and airport issue, 84–85, 87; and business, 87–88; citizens' committee of, on reform, 119; and city council, 124; Civic Problems Committee of, 54; and labor, 54, 88, 123; manager of, 102; and planning, 125; in representative oligarchy, 87–88; Scott-Belleville Committee of, 113–14, 116; and state and federal governments, 116; and United States Chamber of Commerce, 88, 115–16, 123
Belleville Community Council, 55
Belleville Homeowners' Association, 81, 85, 92–93

Belleville Industrial Develop-
ment Corporation, 123–24
Belleville Industrial Development Fund, 124
Belleville National Bank, 41
Belleville *News Democrat,* 67,
87, 105, 129; politics of, 89
Belleville Park District, 53, 64
Belleville Philharmonic Society,
51, 55, 66–67
Belleville Public Library, 98
Belleville Savings Bank, 41
Belleville's New Industry Incorporated, 124
Belleville Township High School
and Junior College, 23, 52;
bond issue to improve and en-
large, 85–86; as community
center, 51–52
Belleville Township High School
and Junior College District,
50, 51–52, 106
Belleville Township High School
District (1916), 64
Belleville Township Junior Col-
lege (1946), 64
Belleville, Township of the City
of, 50; politics in government
of, 102–3
Bi-State Transit Authority (Illi-
nois-Missouri), 108–10
Boards and commissions, permanent, in city government,
97–99
Boilers, manufacture of, 39
Bourbon, whiskey, 37
Boxes, corrugated paper, manufacture of, 39
Breweries, 37, 39; closing of,
during Prohibition, 72
Bricks, manufacture of, 39
Building Code Board of Ap-
peals, 98

Building contractors, in busi-
ness community, 86–87
Buildings, Grounds and Parks
Committee, 96

Cahokia, 20–21
Calhoun, H. B., mayor, 83–84,
90, 93–94, 108; reelection of,
127; reform movement led
by, 69, 89, 120–28
Canteen Township, 50
Carling Brewing Company, 37,
39
Caseyville, 50
Caseyville Township, 50
Catholic(s), 29–35, 89; diocese,
29–30, 34; early German, 29;
elementary schools, 52–53;
high school, 51; and liquor
issue, 35; in politics, 67, 72–
73; property holding of, 35
Cemetery Committee, 96
Centerville Township, 50, 75
Central Trades and Labor Coun-
cil, 43, 90
Chicago Title and Trust Com-
pany, 86–87, 88–89
Cigar industry, 37
Cities of the Prairie: The Metro-
politan Frontier and Ameri-
can Politics (Elazar), 16
Cities of the Prairie series, 4
Citizen's Committee on Flood
Control, 100
Citizen's Committee on Urban
Renewal Development, 100
Citizen's committees, in city gov-
ernment, 99–101
Citizens' Park, 99, 133
Citizen's Traffic Committee, 126
City council, 101; and budget,
94; and Chamber of Com-

merce in reform, 124; committees on, 96–97; first, 61; functions of, 95–97; and labor, 88

City hall (building), 62, 114; new (1961), 82–83, 122

City Plan and Zoning Commission, 100

City townships, 50

Civil community: Belleville as, 6; of Belleville, 20–21; composition of, 4–6; defined, 4

Civil community, governments within: municipal, 49–50; post office, 53, 59; school, 51–53; Scott Air Force Base, 53–54; special district, 53; township, 50–51

Civil Defense Committee, 97, 100

Civil War, and partisan politics, 71

Claims Committee, 96

Clay, 36

Coal mining, 36–37, 39, 42

Coke, 36

Collinsville, 22, 41

Common school districts: #118, 52; Belle Valley, 52; Harmony-Enge, 52; Highmont, 52; Signal Hill, 52; Whiteside, 52

Commuters: to East Saint Louis, 43–44; lack of political activity of, 43–44; to Saint Louis, 40, 43–44, 69

Continental cultural stream, 10–11

Corn, 37

Corrugated paper boxes, manufacture of, 39

County poor home, 61

Courthouse, first, 59

Courthouse Square, city market on, 59

Crime, organized, in American Bottoms, 69

Cultural streams: interrelationships of, 11; modal characteristics of, 11; political cultures and subcultures of, 11–12

Cultural streams, native: Middle, 10–11; Southern, 10–11; Yankee, 10–11

Cultural streams, non-native: Anglo-Canadian, 10–11; Continental, 10–11; Eastern European, 10–11; English, 10–11; French Canadian, 10–11; Irish, 10–11; Jewish, 10–11; Mediterranean, 10–11; North Sea, 10–11

Cultural streams, outside mainstream of American life; Afro-American, 10–11; Hispanic, 11; Oriental, 11

Democratic Party; and Depression, 73; East Saint Louis organization members elected in West End, 67–68; European immigrants in, 72; Germans in, 72; labor in, 73; and repeal, 72–73; in Saint Clair County, 103; Southerners in, 72

Depression: and Democratic Party, 73; federal government projects during, 114–15; and Republican Party, 72–73

Distillery, 37

Dresses, manufacture of, 39

East Belleville, 46

East End, 23, 24, 52, 67

Eastern European cultural stream, 10–11

East Saint Louis, 22, 23, 25, 109, 111, 115, 119, 138–39; civic and business leaders from, to West End, 68; commuters to, 43–44; Democratic organization members from, elected in West End, 67–68; highway network of, 41; immigrants from, 23, 25, 67–68; Negroes from, 68; newspaper from, preferred in East End, 67; political influence of, on township, 104; and reform, 120; urban political machine in, 68–69; vice and crime in, 68–69

Edwardsville, 22, 41, 111

Eisenhower, Dwight D., 89

Elazar, Daniel J.: *Cities of the Prairie: The Metropolitan Frontier and American Politics*, 16; *Toward a Generational Theory of American Politics*, 16

Electric Commissioners, Board of, 98

English cultural stream, 10–11

English, immigrants of, origin, 28–29

English Methodist Church, 29

Evangelical Church (German Protestant), 29, 32–33

Fairview Station, 107

Federalism, American, place of Belleville in, 16

Fields, Alvin, East Saint Louis political "boss," 75; and personal property taxes, 131–32; support of, by businessmen, 89–90

Finance and Audit Committee, 96, 97

Fire departments: interrelated, within civil community, 53, 108; municipal, 53; semi-professional, 63; volunteer, 56, 61, 63

First National Bank of Belleville, 41, 86, 125–26

First Presbyterian Church (Yankee), 29, 31–32

Flood control, 141; federal assistance in, 115; Illinois assistance in, 115; on Richland Creek, 100, 130–31

Flour mills, 39

"Foreign policy," 66, 68–70

Foundries, 38

Freeburg, 55

French Canadian cultural stream, 10–11

Frontiers in American historical development: as experienced by Belleville, 7–9; metropolitan-technological, 7, 135–36; rural-land, 6; urban-industrial, 6–7

Full Gospel Church, 30

Fundamentalist Protestant(s), 33–34, 141; Full Gospel Church, 30; Pentecostal Church, 30

Furnaces, industrial, manufacture of, 39

Gambling, elimination of, in reform, 120

Garments, manufacture of, 39

Gas, natural, 36

Gas and Plumbing Code Board of Appeals, 98

Generational theory of political behavior, 16–18; as applied to Belleville, 17–18

German(s): architecture, influence of, on, 25–26; breweries, 37; cigar industry, 37; Catholicism, early, 29; as citizens, 67; in Democratic Party, 71; and labor unions, 43; and early libraries, 43, 60–61; as mayors, 71; Protestantism, early, 29, 32; in Republican Party, 71–72; and early schools, 43, 61; and urban order, 139

Ghettos, urban, 136

Government: local, and politics, 75–76; relations between city and county, 76

Governments within civil community; municipal, 49–50; post office, 53; schools, 51–53; Scott Air Force Base, 53–54; special districts, 53; township, 50–51

Grocery stores: early prohibition of, 59; establishment of private, 63

Harmony-Enge (common school) District, 52

Health, Board of, 98, 99

Health, public, services, state regulation of, 110

Health and Sanitation Committee, 96

Highmont (common school) District, 52

Highways, 41; Illinois assistance in improving, 109–10; improvements of, by city, 64; and local governments, 64; State Highway #460, 41, 110. *See also* Roads.

Homeowners' associations, 24–25, 81, 85, 92–93

Hospitals; Memorial (Protestant), 34; Saint Elizabeth's (Catholic), 34

Illinois, state of, 58, 108; becomes state, 60; and Belleville, 109–12; Budgetary Commission of, 110; political party organization in, 27

Illinois Budgetary Commission, 110

Illinois Central Railroad, 40

Illinois Cities and Villages Act, 61, 63

Illinois Education Association, 105

Illinois Power Company, 123

Immigrants, 27; English, 28–29; German, 25–26, 29; Southern, 24, 26, 28, 29; Yankee, 29

Incorporation of Belleville: as city, 61, 63; as village, 60

Individualistic political subculture, 12–15

Irish cultural stream, 10–11

Jewish cultural stream, 10–11, 30

Jews, 30–31, 34–35; as business leaders, 35; as retail merchants, 89

Johnson, Lyndon B., 135–36

Judiciary and Legislative Committee, 96

Juvenile delinquency, 67

Kaskaskia River, 41, 115
Kaskaskia Valley Association, 115
Kennedy, John F., 135–36
Kern, Fred J., mayor, 93

Labor: in Democratic Party, 73; and federal projects during Depression, 114; force, 42; and mayor, 83–84, 93, 128, 129; in representative oligarchy, 80. See also Unions, labor.
Land survey, federal, 113
Latin peasant movement, 71
Lebanon, 108
Legislative Committee, 101
Libraries: early, 43, 60; first public, 64; Belleville Public Library, 98
Library Association, 60–61
Library Board, 98, 99
Limestone, 36
Liquor, 35; and tavern control in reform, 121, 128
"Local Government as an Ecology of Games" (Long), 141
Long, Norton: "Local Government as an Ecology of Games," 141
Louisville and Nashville Railroad, 24, 40
Lutheran Church, 32–33; elementary parochial school of, 53

Machine politics, in East Saint Louis, 68–69
Machine tool patterns and dies, manufacture of, 39
Madison County, 41, 50, 111, 124

Manufacturing, 37–39. See also names of individual industries and products.
Market, city, 59–60, 63
Master Sewer Plan Financing, Advisory Committee on, 100
Mayor: appointments by, 76, 97–99; and budget, 94; first, 61; function of, 93–95; Germans as, 71; as head of ticket, 73; and labor, 93; office of, weak, 93; religion of, 93; salary of, 93. See also Calhoun, H. B.; Munie, Jerome J.; Nichols, Charles; Tieman, Ernest.
Mediterranean cultural stream, 10–11
Memorial Hospital (Protestant), 34
Menard State Penitentiary, 128
Merchants, retail, Jews as, 89
Methodist Church, English, 29, 33
Metropolitan-technological frontier, 7
Middle cultural stream, 10–11, 29; individualistic political subculture out of, 12
Millet system, Near Eastern, 31
Milling, 37
Millstadt, 55
Mississippi River, 20, 36, 40, 49
Missouri, state of, 108
Moralistic political subculture, 12
Municipalities, as government within civil community, 49–50
Munie, Jerome J., mayor, sheriff, warden, 76–77, 83–84, 94, 128; illness of, during term as mayor, 84, 129; and labor,

83–84, 128; reforms of, 128–29

Nail mills, 38
Near Eastern Millet system, 31
Negroes, 35–36; in American Bottoms, 68; from East Saint Louis, 68; lack of gain of, 140; and public housing, 130; in urban ghettos, 136
Neighborhood improvement associations, 55–56
New Athens, 41, 115
New Deal, 73
New Frontier, 135–36
Nichols, Charles, alderman, mayor, 84, 89, 90, 93–94, 108, 134, 139; as first full-time mayor, 129; reforms of, 128–32
Northeastern sectionalism, 15
North Sea cultural stream, 10–11
Northwestern University, 125

O'Fallon, 50, 51, 53, 108
O'Fallon Township, 51
Oligarchy as political control: and autocracy, 79; multiple-element, 79; representative, 79; single-element, 78–79. *See also* Representative oligarchy
Ordinance and License Committee, 96

Parent-Teachers Associations (PTA), 85; in school politics, 105–6
Parking problem, 125–26, 128
Parochial elementary schools: Catholic, 52–53; Lutheran, 53
Pentecostal Church, 30

Personal property taxes, 131–32
Planning Commission (1961), 65, 125
Platting as city: private, 58; of West Belleville, 62
Playground and Recreation Board, 99
Police and Fire Commissioners, Board of, 97, 98, 99
Police and Fire Committee, 97
Police department; cooperation of, with other local departments, 109; establishment of, 63; reform of, 120–21; suicide of chief of, 119; vigil of, against syndicate, 69
Police Pension Board, 97, 98
Political behavior, generational theory of, 16–18
Political culture, of Belleville, 12–15
Political parties, local: candidate selection by, 73; changes of names of, 73; in city politics, 75–76; movement from party to party in, 74; organization of, 73; organization of, in Illinois, 27; organization of, in Saint Clair County, 27
Political parties, national, role of, in local politics, 74–75
Political subcultures of cultural streams: individualistic, 12; moralistic, 12; traditionalistic, 12
Politicians, in representative oligarchy, 91–92
Polyarchy as political control: chaotic, 80; fragmented, 80
Post office: first, 59–60, 112; first permanent, building, 64; as government within civil community, 53

Precincts of wards, 26–27; redistricting of, 126–27

Presbyterian Church (Yankee), 29, 31–33

Price, Melvin, Congressman, 114

Professionals in city government, 101–2

Prohibition: closing of breweries during, 72; and Democratic Party, 72–73; and Republican Party, 72–73

Prostitution, elimination of, during reform, 121

Protestant(s): early German, 29; early Southern, 28; Fundamentalist, 30; and liquor issue, 35; in politics, 67; realtors and bankers, 89. *See also* names of individual denominations and sects

Public Relations and Personnel Committee, 96

Railroads: Illinois Central Railroad, 40; Louisville and Nashville Railroad, 24, 40; Southern Railway System, 40, 123

Realtors: in business community, 86–87; and Belleville Homeowners' Association, 92; as Protestants, 89

Recreation department, expansion of, 133

Reform: annexation of suburban areas in, 126, 131; background to, 118–19; Calhoun in, 120–27; Chamber of Commerce and business-agricultural programs in, 124; Chamber of Commerce and city council in, 124; Chamber of Commerce and labor in, 123; citizens' committee in, 119;

city hall, new building for, in, 122; city services, improvement of, in, 121–22; civilian employees, improvement in caliber of, in, 121; cultural facilities, improvement of, in, 133; demolition of unsafe buildings in, 130; downtown beautification in, 133; East Saint Louis element in, 120; flood control in, 130; gambling, elimination of organized, in, 120; industrial development in, 123–24; liquor and tavern control in, 121; parking problems in, 125–26; Planning Commission in, 125; in police department, 120–21; prostitution, elimination of, in, 121; public facilities, construction of, in, 133; recreation department, expansion of, in, 133; redistricting wards and precincts in, 126–27, 129; school expansion in, 132; sewer expansion in, 126, 129; social welfare services, improvement of, in, 133; traffic control plan in, 125; urban renewal in, 130; zoning in, 125, 129

Reformed churches (German), 32

Religion: and local politics, 27–35; of mayor, 93; in representative oligarchy, 80; and school politics, 105–6. *See also* names of individual churches, denominations, and sects

Rent control, 92

Repeal: and Democratic Party, 72–73; and Republican Party, 72

Representative oligarchy: and airport issue, 84–85; business in, 80, 86–90; and city hall heating plant, 83; divide and re-form, ability of, to, 84–86; labor in, 80, 90–91; mayoral campaigns in, 83–84; opponents of, 92–93; politicians in, 80, 90–92; religion in, 80; and school bond issue, 85–86; screening and recruitment of candidates for office by, 83; and sewer construction program, 80–82; and urban renewal, 85

Republican Party: and Depression, 72–73; Germans in, 71–72; and Nichols, 129; and Prohibition, 72–73; and Repeal, 72; in Saint Clair County, 103

Richland Creek, 23, 62; flood control on, 100, 130–31

Roads: Saint Louis Road, 24, 39–40, 49; toll, 40, 64. *See also* Highways

Rural-land frontier, 6; establishment of culture patterns during, 9

Saint Clair County, 20, 41, 50, 58, 75–77, 109, 124, 128, 131–32; and city government, 76–77; political party organization in, 27, 75; politics in, 103; township organization of, 63–64

Saint Clair National Bank, 41

Saint Clair Township, 50–51; government of, 104

Saint Elizabeth's Hospital (Catholic), 34

Saint Louis, 9, 20, 22, 38, 39–40; air facilities of, 40–41; commuters to, 40, 43–44, 69; police department, 121; Standard Metropolitan Statistical Area (SMSA), 3; transportation network of, 41, 108–9; water facilities of, 40

Saint Louis Road, 24, 39–40, 49

Sand, 36

Savings and loan associations, 41–42

School bond issue, 85–86

School districts: #116, 105–6; Belle Valley (119), 52, 106; Belleville Township High School (1916), 64; Belleville Township High School and Junior College, 50, 51–52, 106; Harmony-Enge, 52; Highmont, 52; Signal Hill (118), 52, 106; Whiteside, 52

Schools: Catholic high, 51; common, 52; district (1856), 62; early, 43, 59; expansion of, 132; first, 58–59; as government within civil community, 51–53; parochial elementary, 52–53; politics in, 104–7; public high, 51

Scott Air Force Base, 39, 43–44, 55, 70, 108, 111–13, 119; as government within civil community, 53–54; Scott-Belleville Committee regarding, 113–14, 116

Scott-Belleville Committee, 113–14, 116

Sectionalism, American: influence of, on Belleville, 15–16; Northeastern, 15; Southern, 15; Western, 15

Sewage Disposal and Sewer Lines Committee, 97

Sewer construction program: federal government aid in, 115; as indication of representative oligarchy, 80–82; in reform, 126

Shelton Gang (criminal group), 119

Shiloh, 50, 53, 108

Shiloh Valley, 51

Shiloh Valley Township, 51

Shoes, manufacturing of, 39

Signal Hill, 52, 53

Signal Hill (common school) District (118), 52, 106

Signal Hill Fire District, 53

Smith, Alfred E., 72–73

SMSA. *See* Standard Metropolitan Statistical Area.

Social welfare services, improvement in, 133

Sonic booms, 109, 114

Southern Baptist, early, congregation, 28

Southern cultural stream, 10–11, 28, 29; traditionalistic political subculture out of, 112

Southerners: architecture, influence of, on, 24, 26; in Democratic Party, 72; original settlement by, 26, 28, 58–59; whiskey preference of, 37

Southern Illinois University, 111, 130

Southern Protestantism, early, 28

Southern sectionalism, 15

Southern Railway System, 40, 123

Southside Improvement Association, 56

Special districts: Belleville Park District, 53; Signal Hill Fire District, 53; as government within civil community, 53

Standard Metropolitan Statistical Area (SMSA), 3–4

Stencil machines, manufacturing of, 39

Stookey Township, 50–51

Stoves, manufacturing of, 39

Streets, importance of, in social organization, 22–25

Streets and Bridges Committee, 97

Subdivisions, unincorporated, 56–57

Suburbs, as product of metropolitan frontier, 136

Swansea, 49–50, 52, 53, 104, 105, 108, 116

Syndicate. *See* Crime, organized

Tacks, manufacturing of, 39

Teachers' union, 90–91, 129; in school politics, 105–6

Tieman, Ernest, mayor, 119–20

Tie cutters, manufacturing of, 39

Topography, influence of: on place of residence, 57; on precinct organization, 26; on settlement and growth of Belleville, 20–25

Touchette, Elmer, 75, 90

Toward a Generational Theory of American Politics (Elazar), 16

Townships: Belleville, of the City of, 50, 63; Canteen, 50; Caseyville, 50; Centerville, 50; O'Fallon, 51; Saint Clair, 50–51; Shiloh Valley, 51; Stookey, 50–51; city, 50; as government within civil community, 50–51; organization adopted by Saint Clair County, 63; school politics in, 104–7

Traditionalistic political subculture, 12–15

Traffic and Parking Meters Committee, 97

Traffic control plan, 125

Transportation facilities, 39–41; Bi-State Transit Authority in, 108–9, 110; state regulation of, 109–10

Trousers, manufacturing of, 39

Unemployment, 42

Union Label Committee, 83, 90

Unions, labor, 85; and Chamber of Commerce, 54, 88, 123; coal miners', 91; early, 37, 43; of political employees, 15, 90–91; present, 42–43; and reform, 123; in representative oligarchy, 90–91; teachers', 90–91, 105–6. *See also* Labor.

United Church of Christ, 32

U.S. Army Corps of Engineers, 100

U.S. Bureau of Public Roads, 109

U.S. Chamber of Commerce, and Belleville Chamber of Commerce, 88, 115–16, 123

U.S. Federal Bureau of Investigation (FBI), 121

U.S. federal government: aid in Kaskaskia waterways project, 115; aid in sewer projects and flood control, 115; in civil community, 111–16; land

survey, 113; projects during Depression, 114–15

U.S. Federal Housing Administration (FHA), 115

U.S. Military Air Transport Service, 113

U.S. Soil Conservation Service, 100

U.S. Works Progress Administration (WPA), 73, 114–15

Urban-industrial frontier, 6–7

Urban renewal: under Munie, 129; under Nichols, 129; and representative oligarchy, 85

Utilities, state regulation of, 110

Utilities Board of Appeals, 98

Utilities Committee, 96

Wards, 26–27, 61; redistricting of, 126–27

Water facilities: on Kaskaskia River, 41, 115; of Mississippi River, 36, 40, 49; of Saint Louis, 40

West Belleville, 23, 46; platting of, 62

West End, 23, 24–25, 46–49, 52, 67–69, 75

Western sectionalism, 15

Whiskey, bourbon, 37

Whiteside (common school) District, 52

World War I, and partisan politics, 72

Yankee cultural stream, 10–11, 29; moralistic political subculture out of, 12

Yankee immigrants, 29, 31–32, 58–59, 63

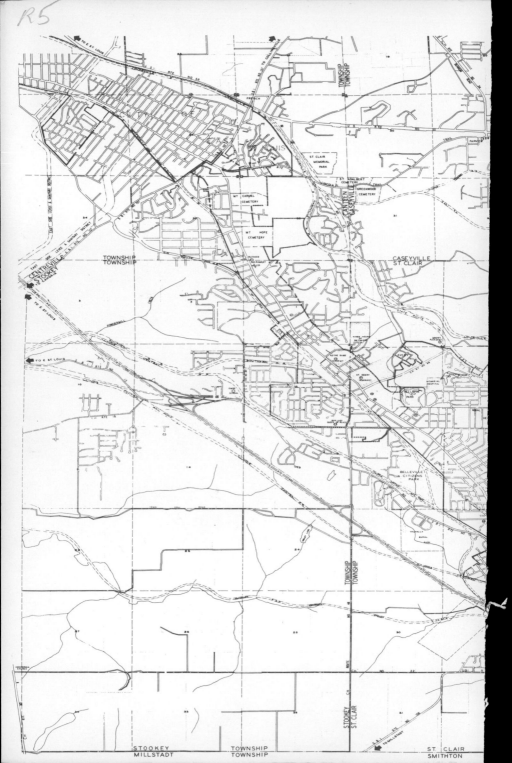